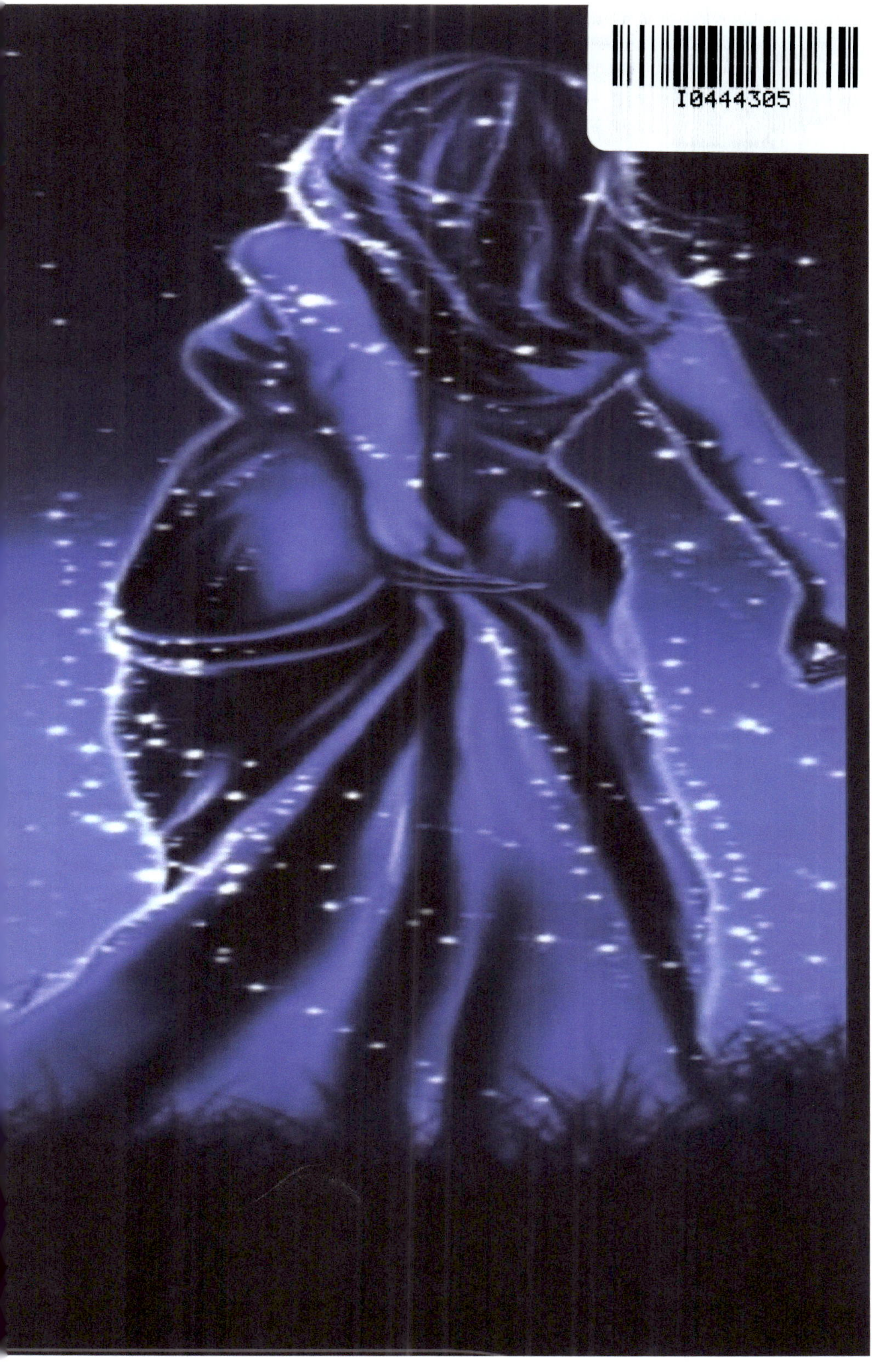

I0444305

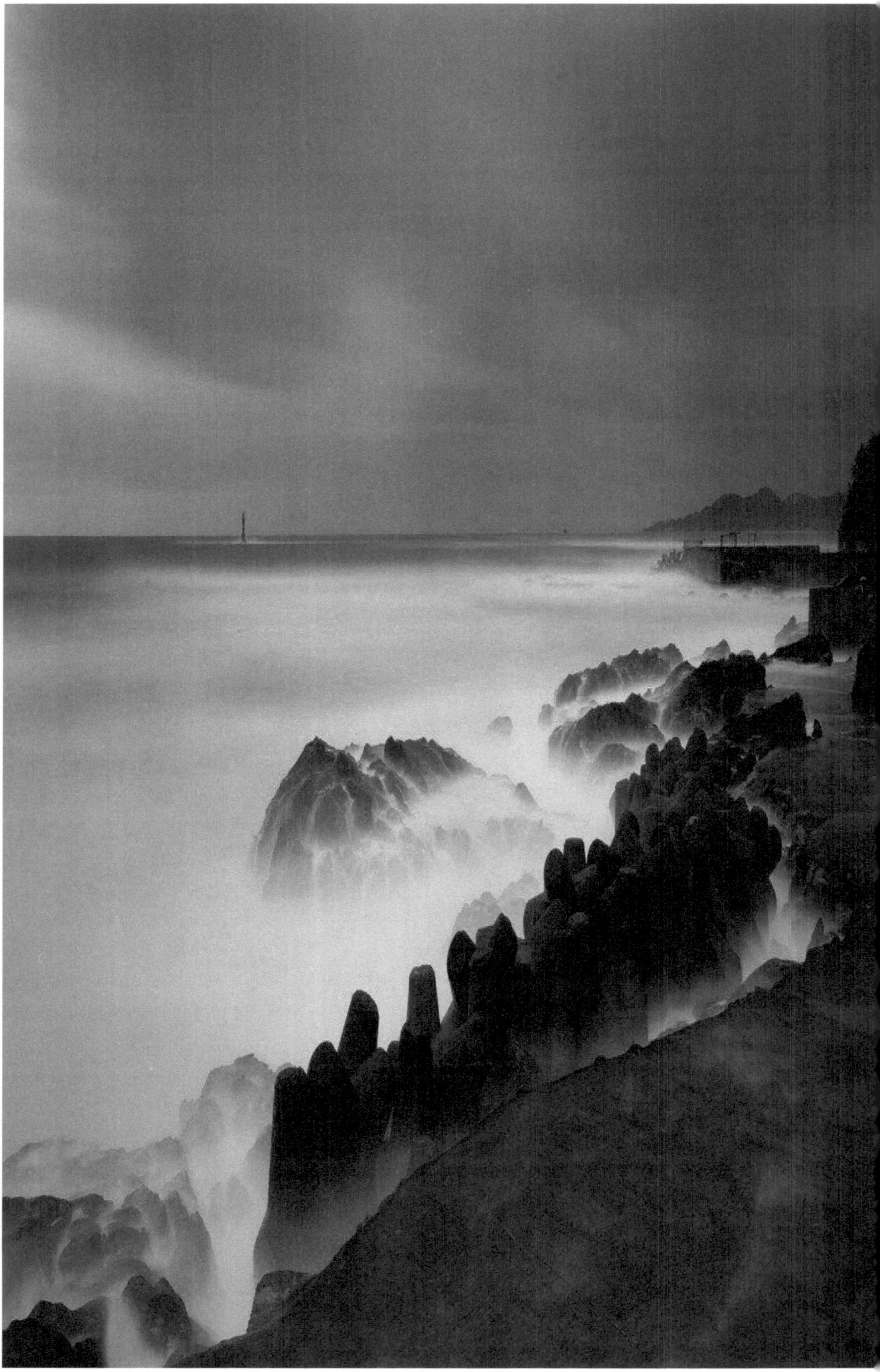

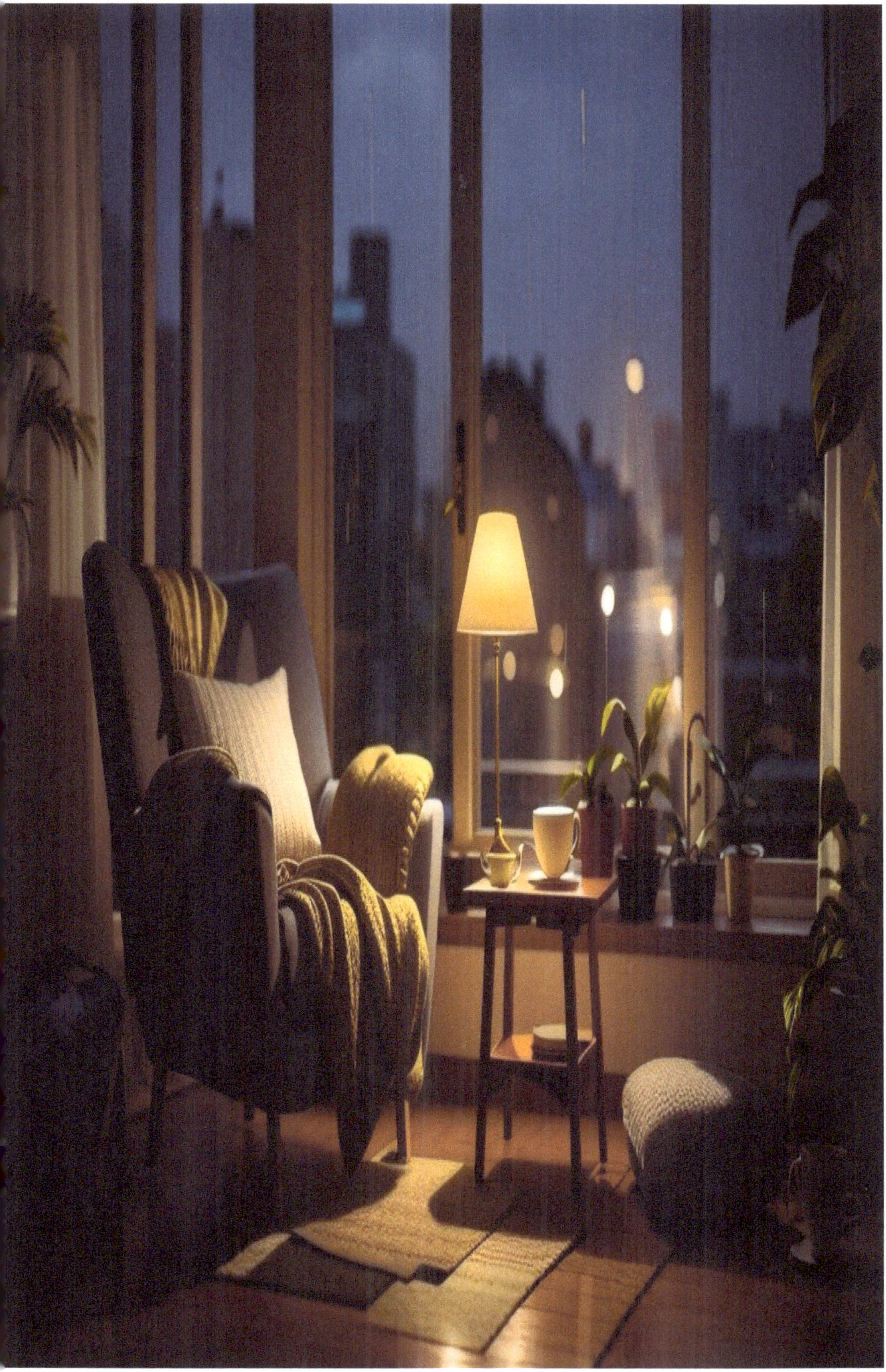

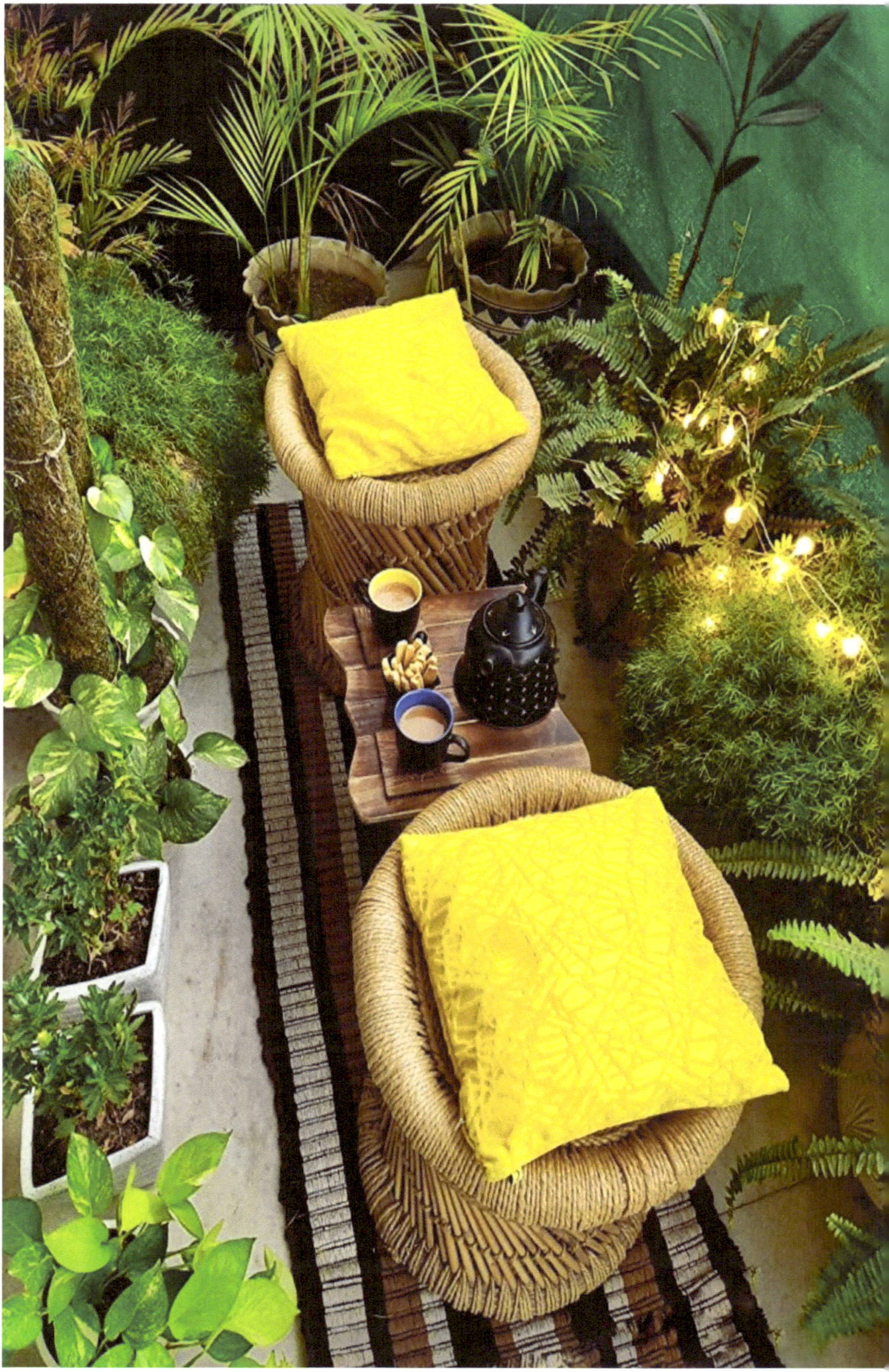

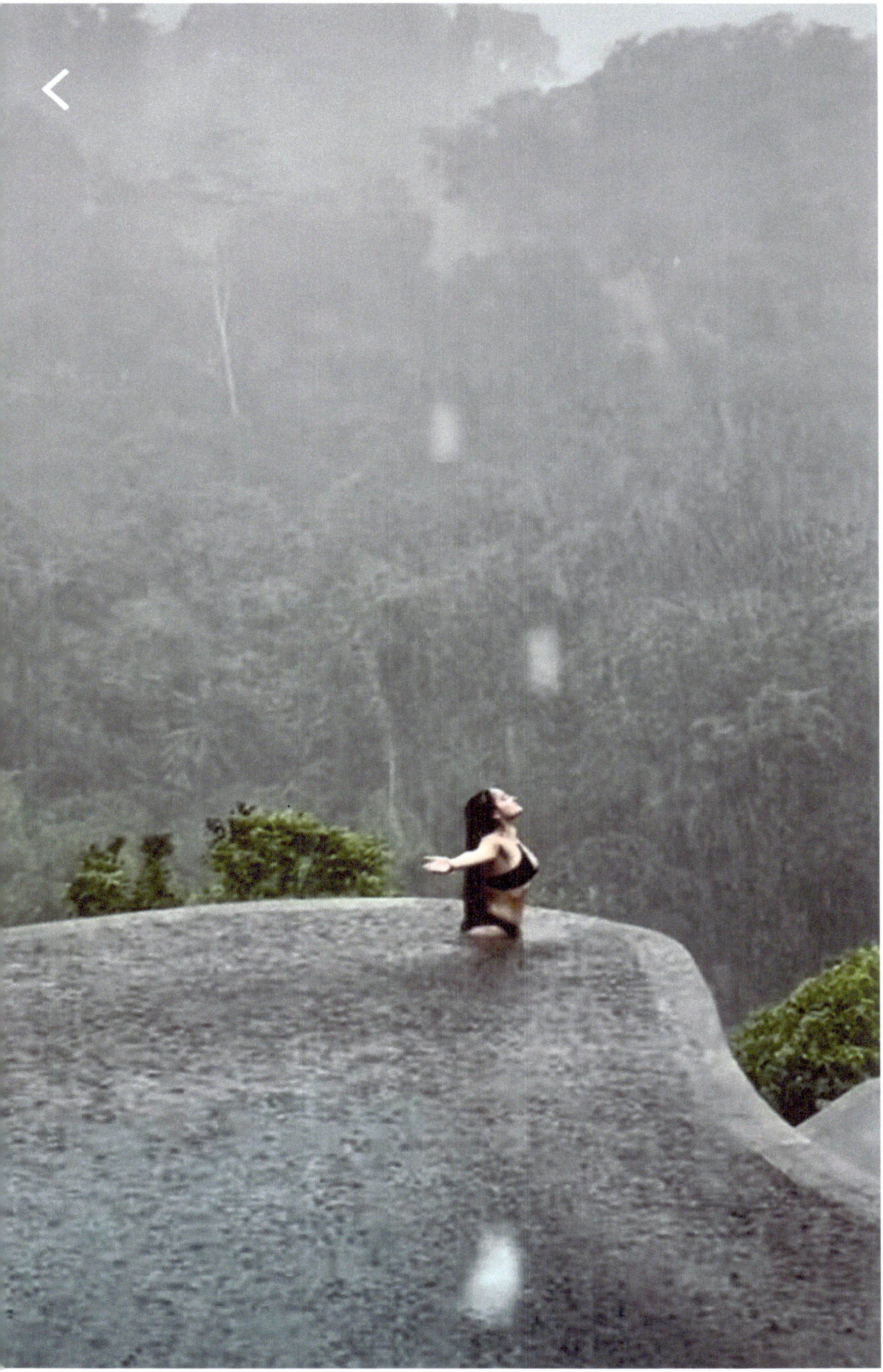

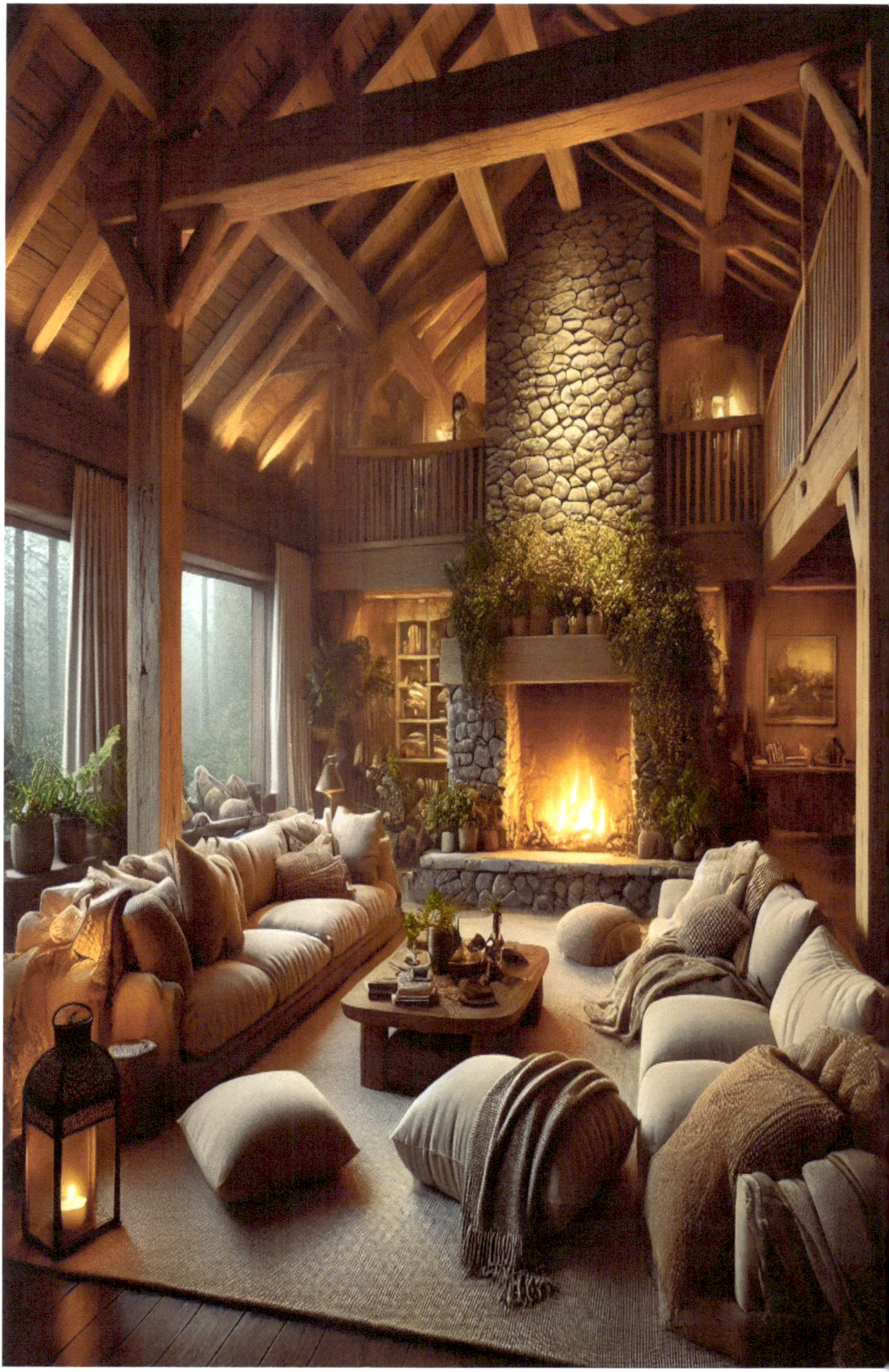

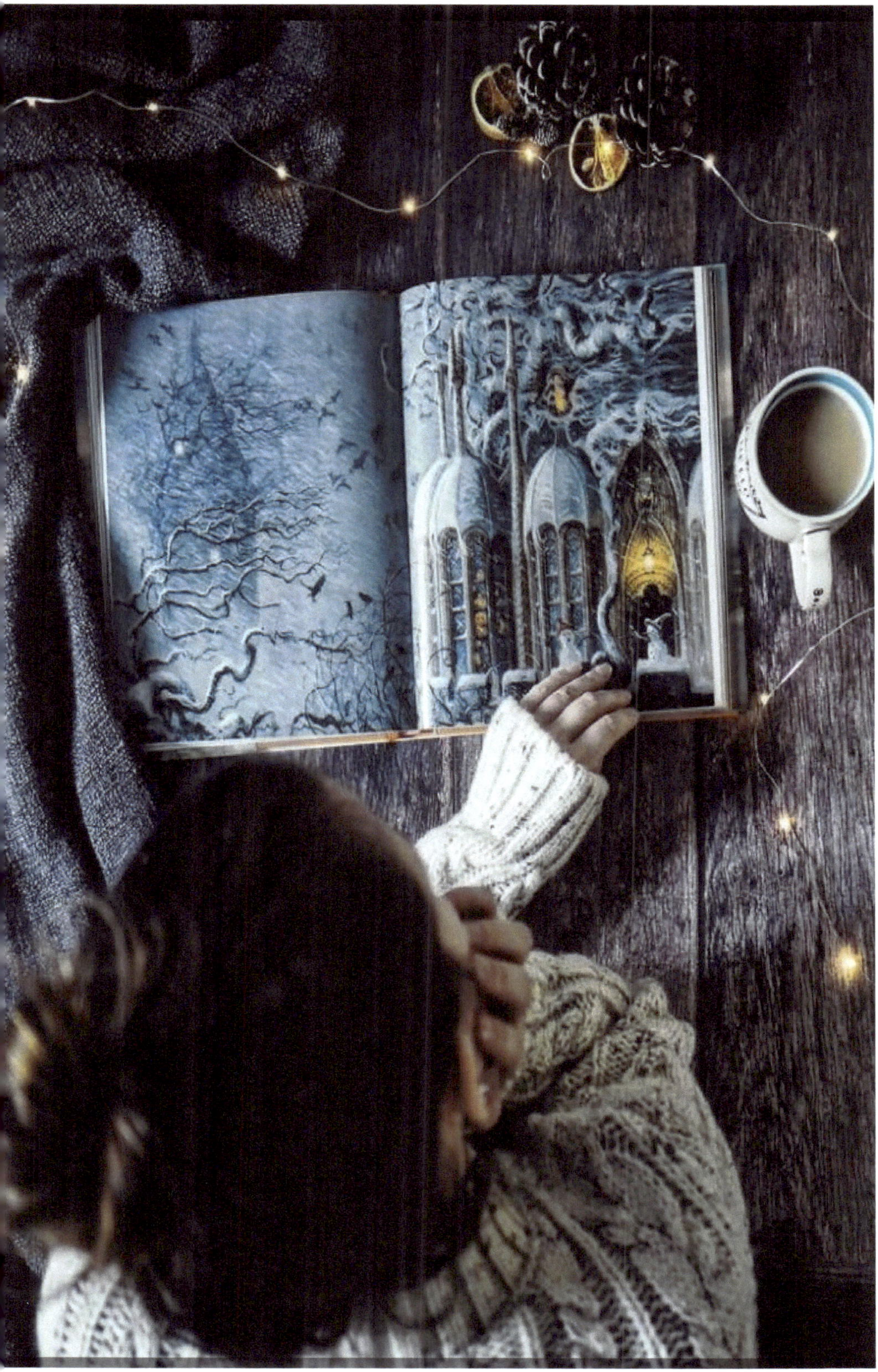

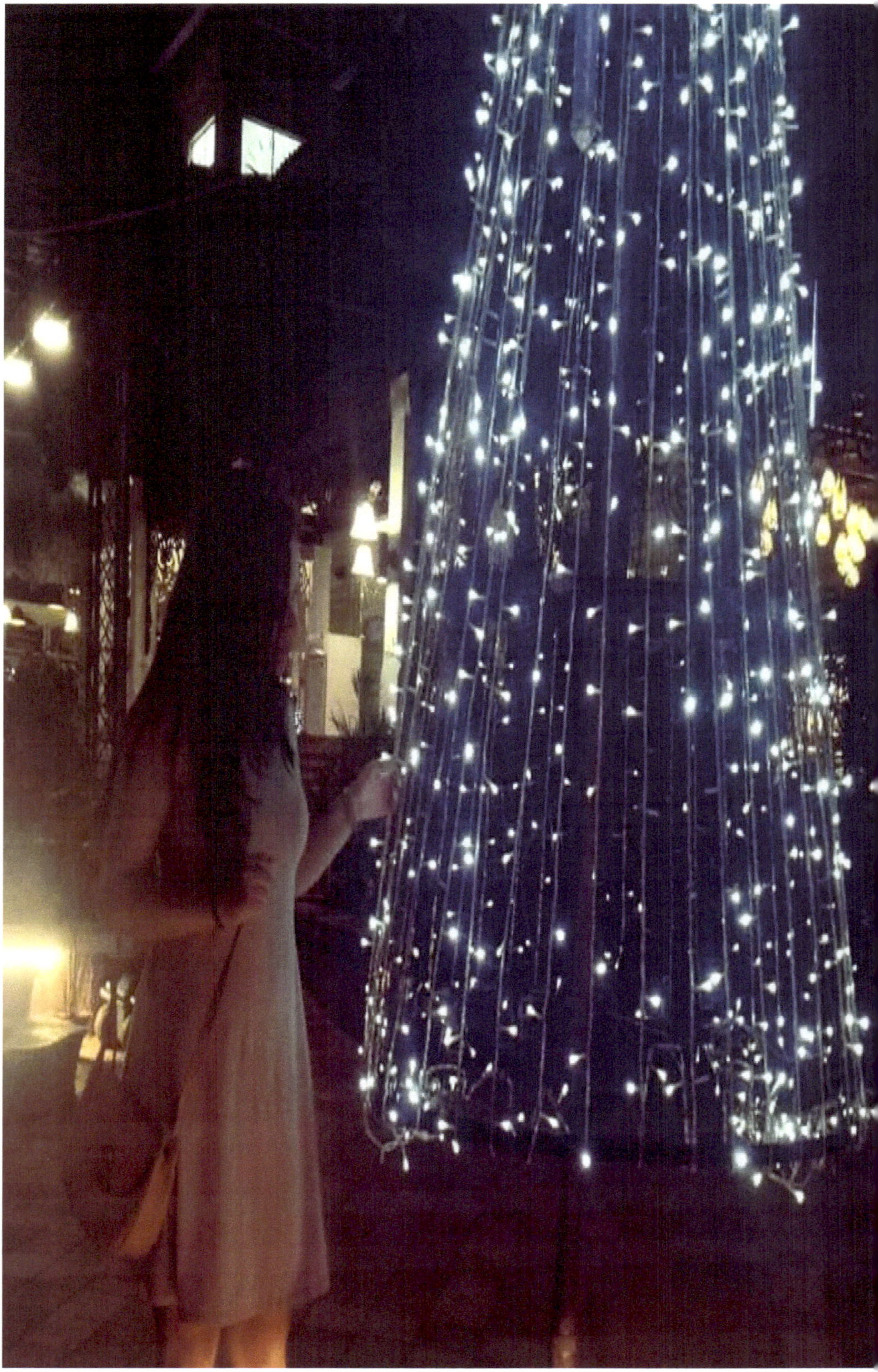

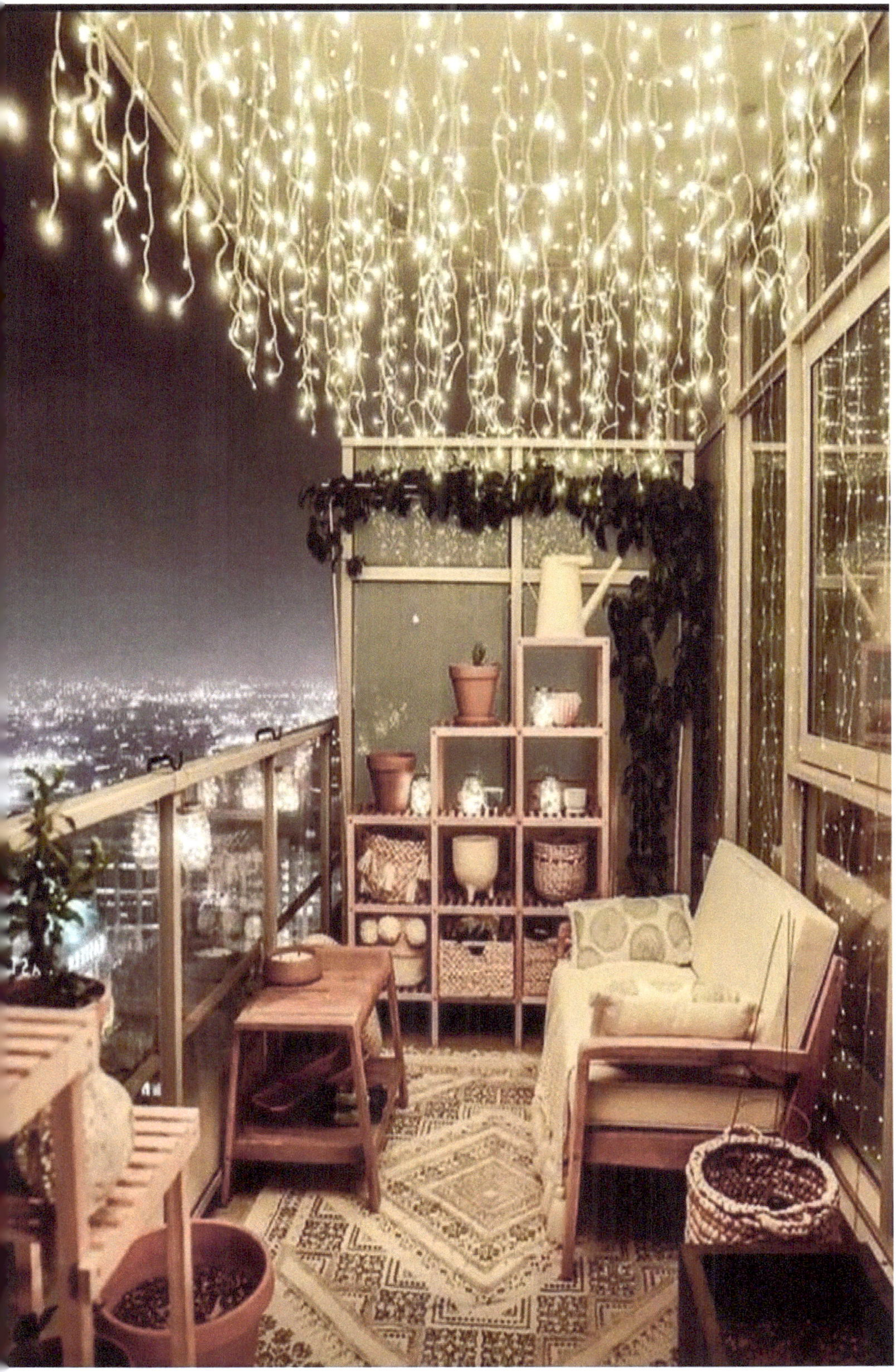

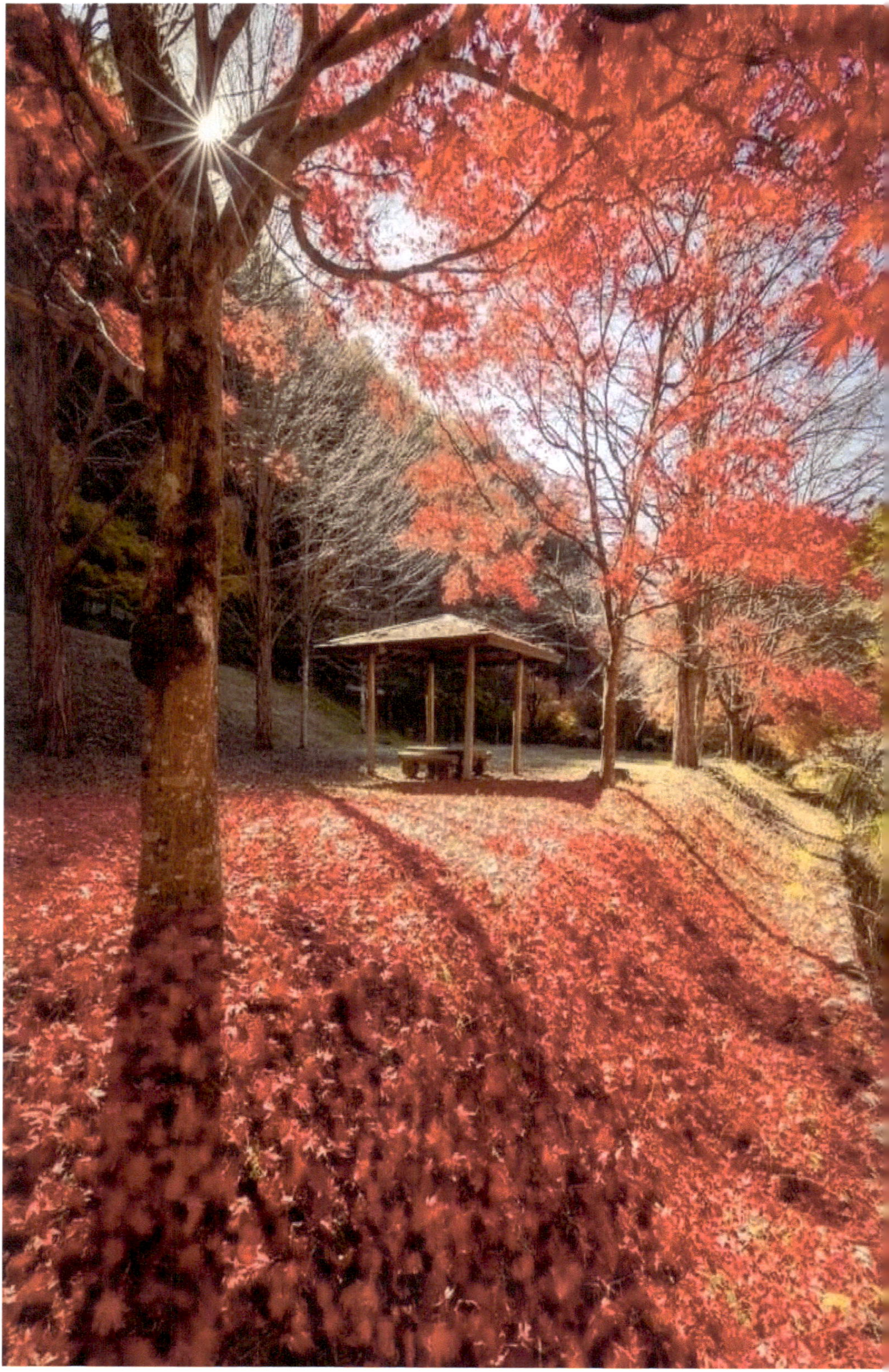

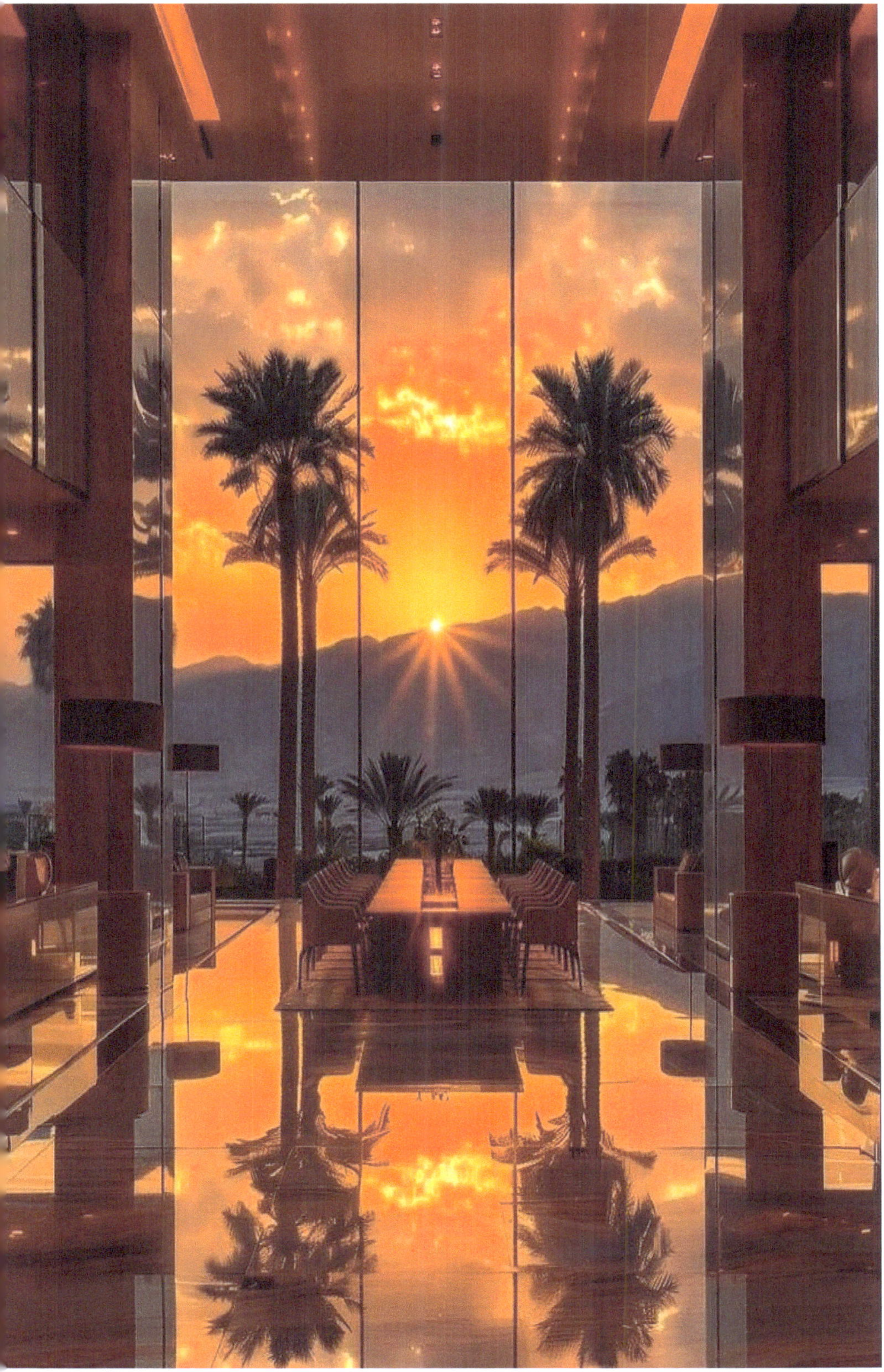

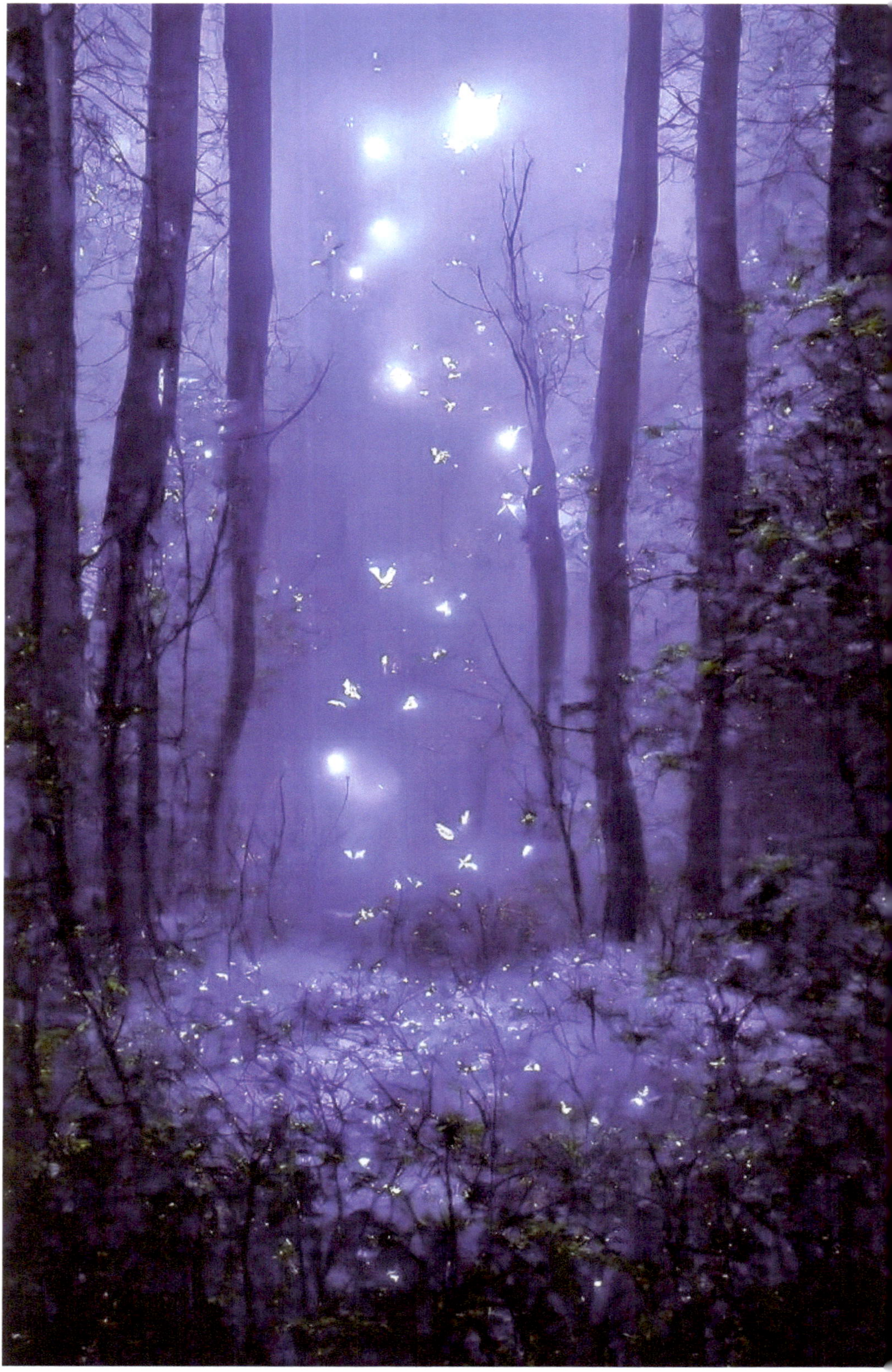

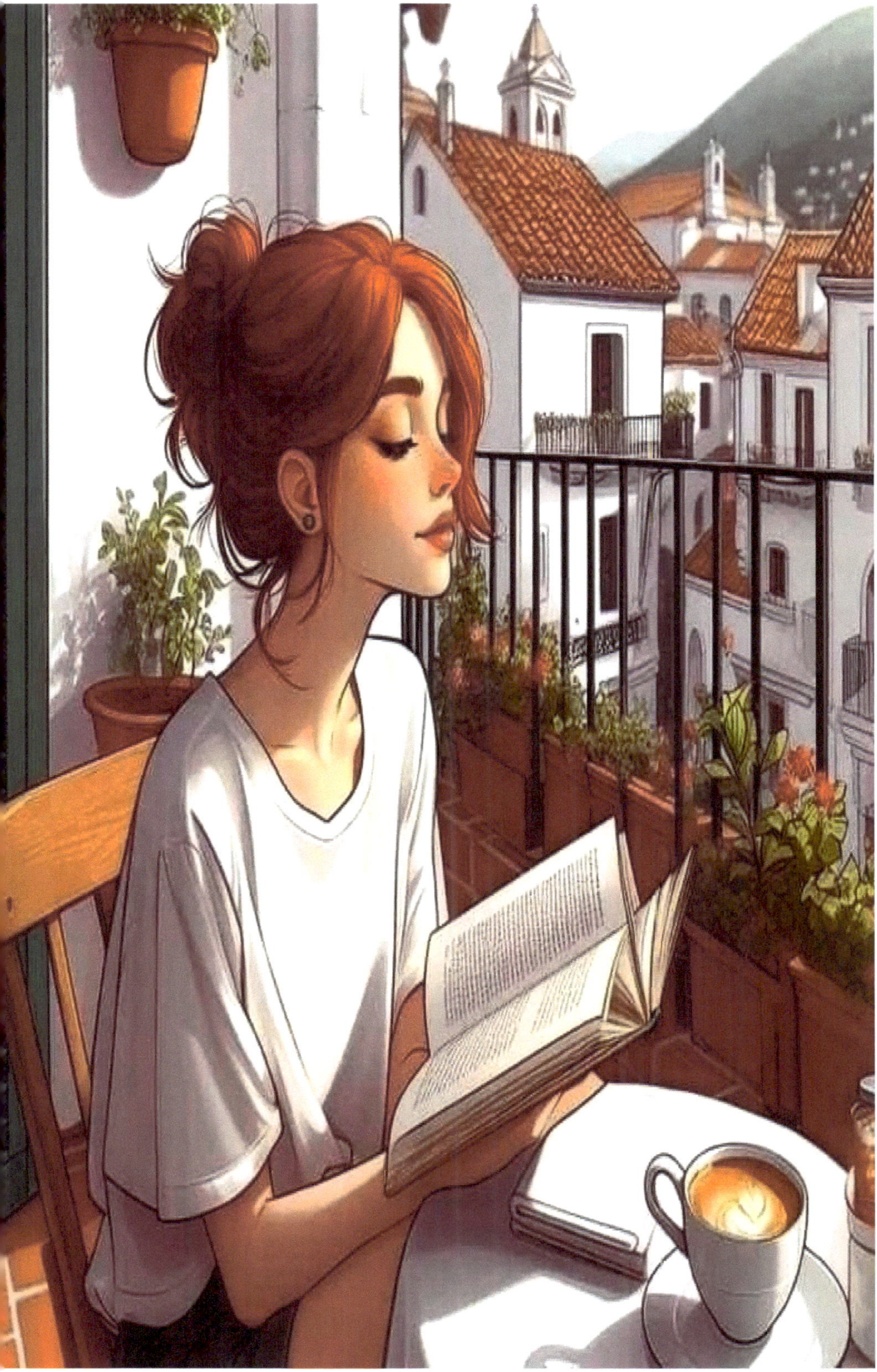

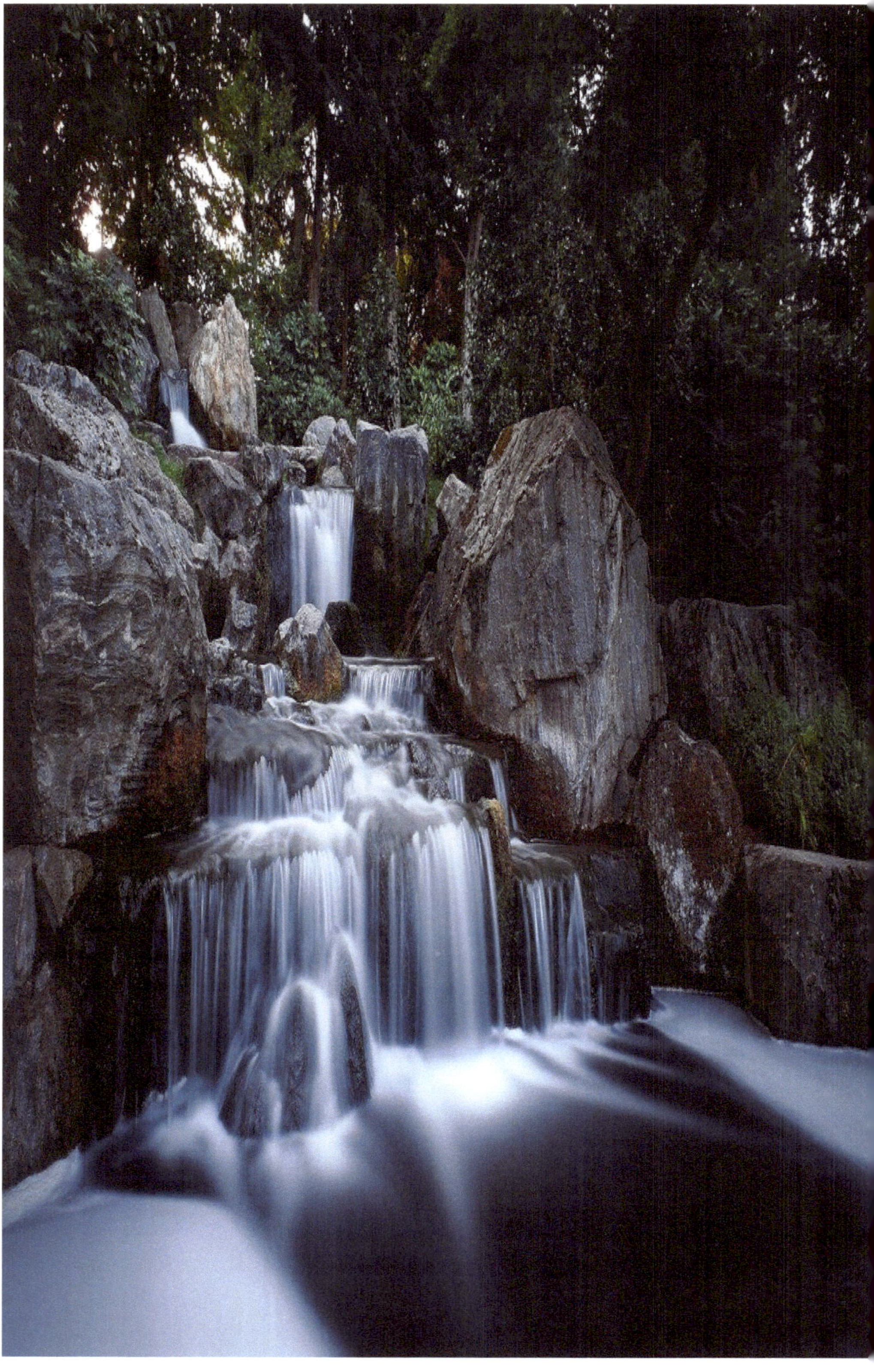

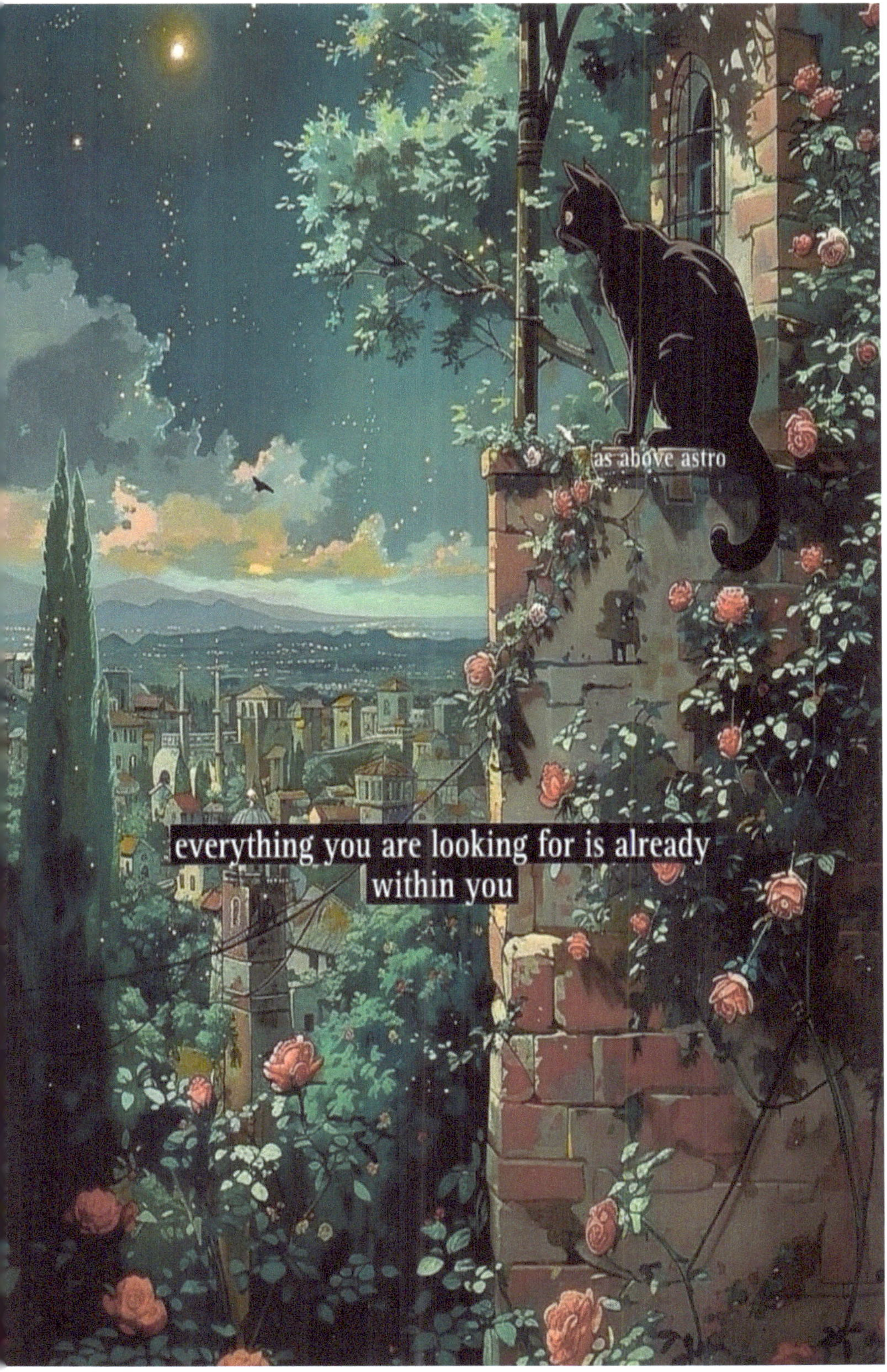
as above astro
everything you are looking for is already
within you

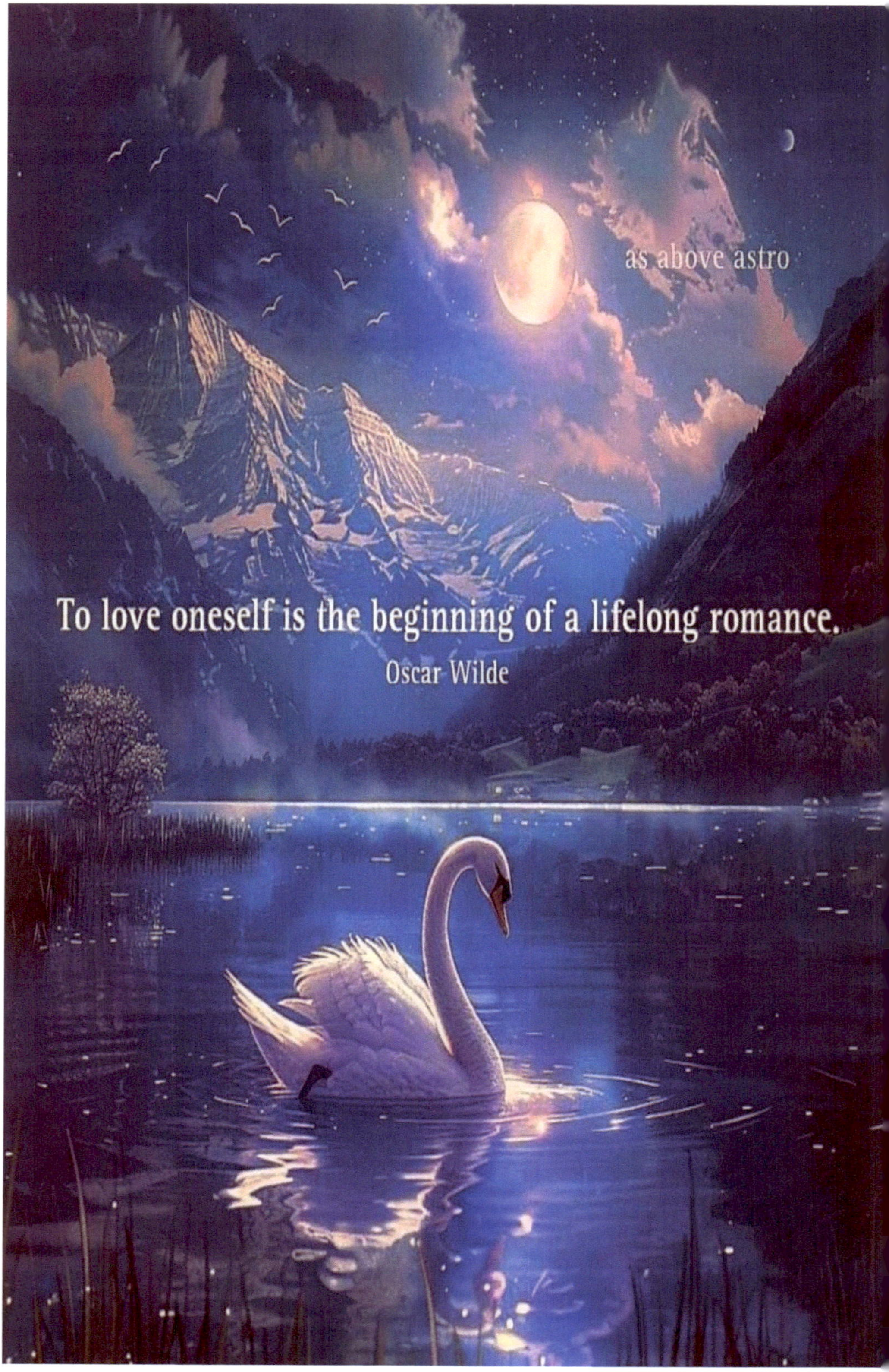
as above astro
To love oneself is the beginning of a lifelong romance.
Oscar Wilde

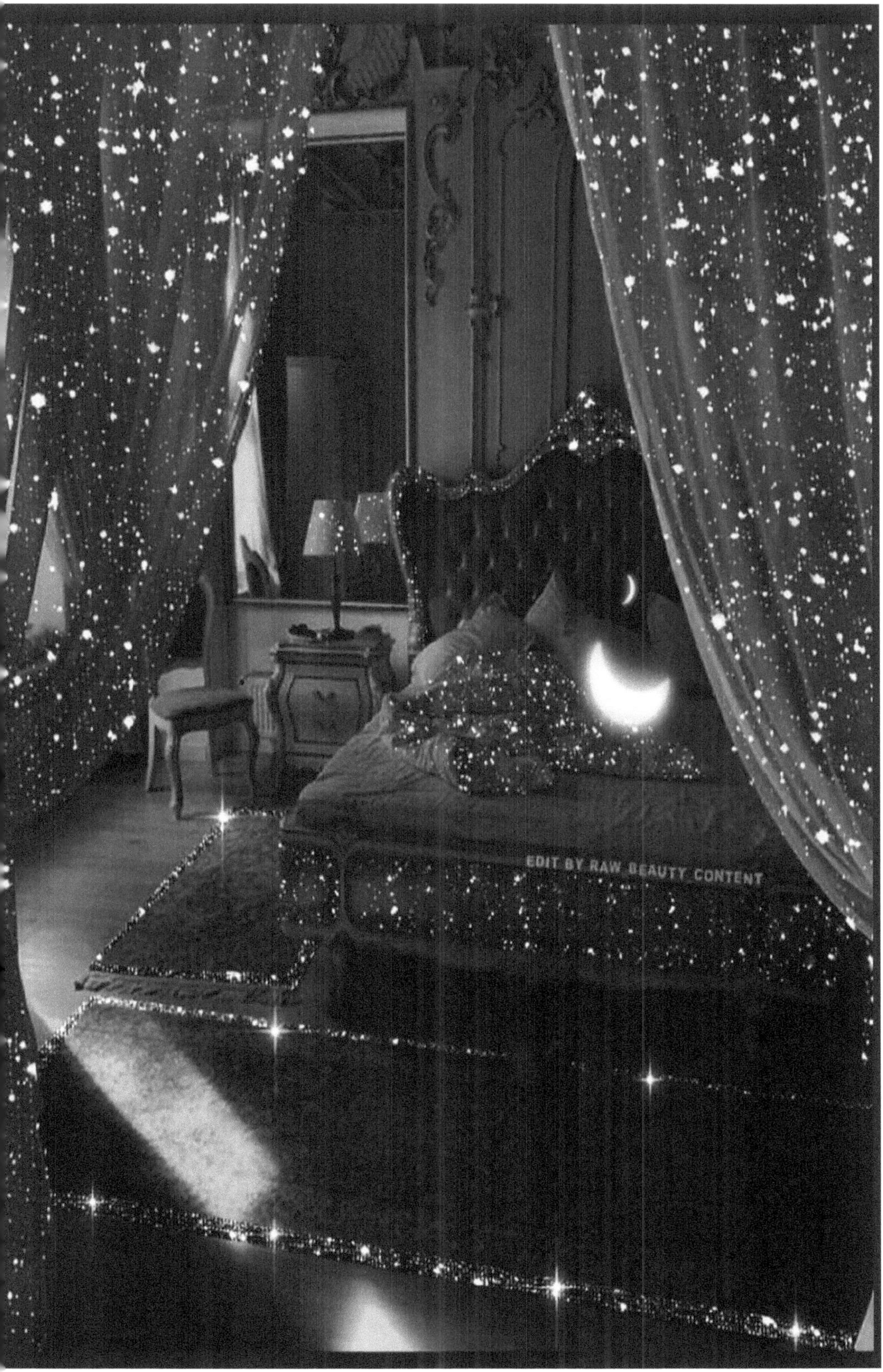
EDIT BY RAW_BEAUTY_CONTENT

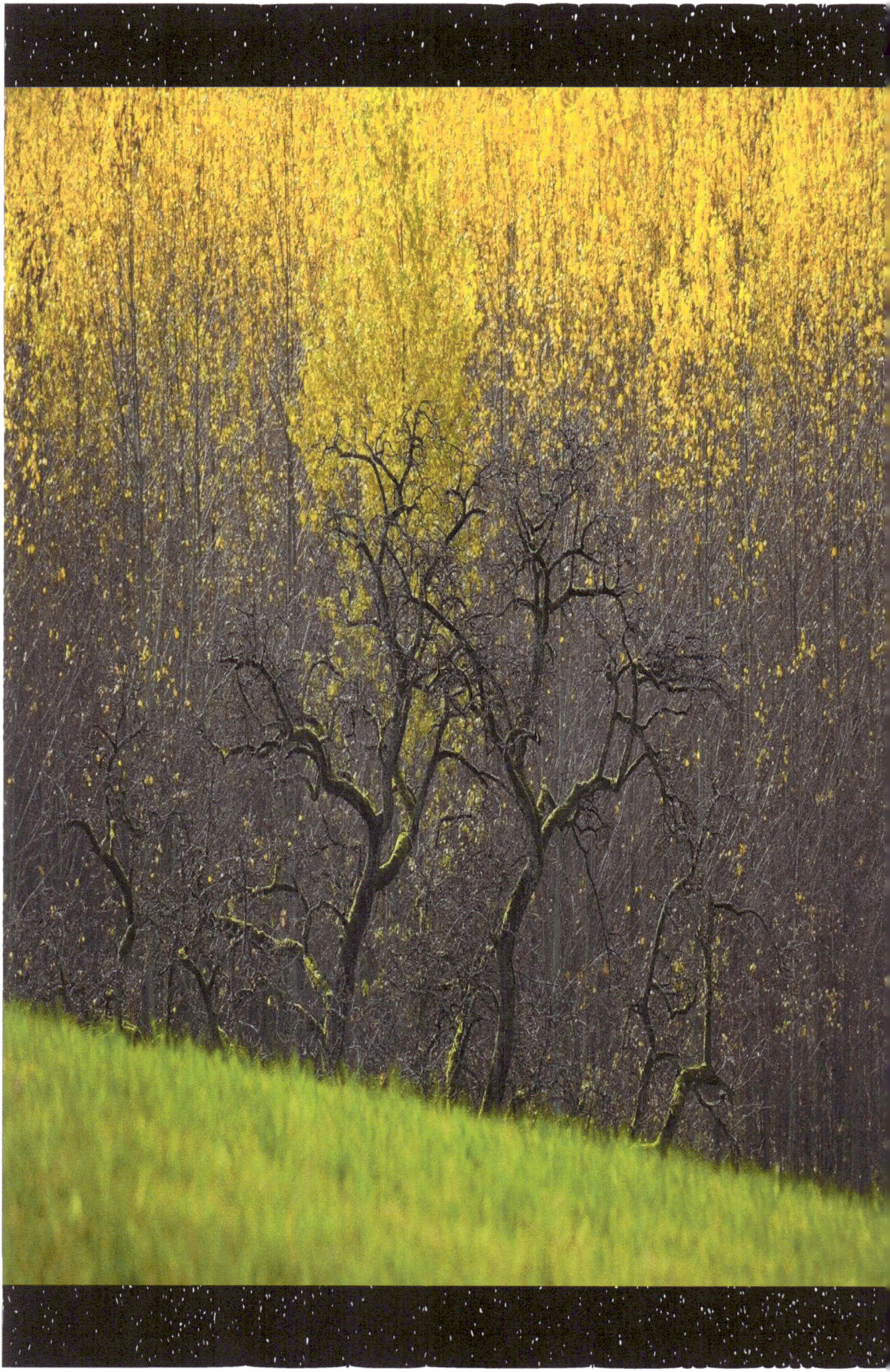

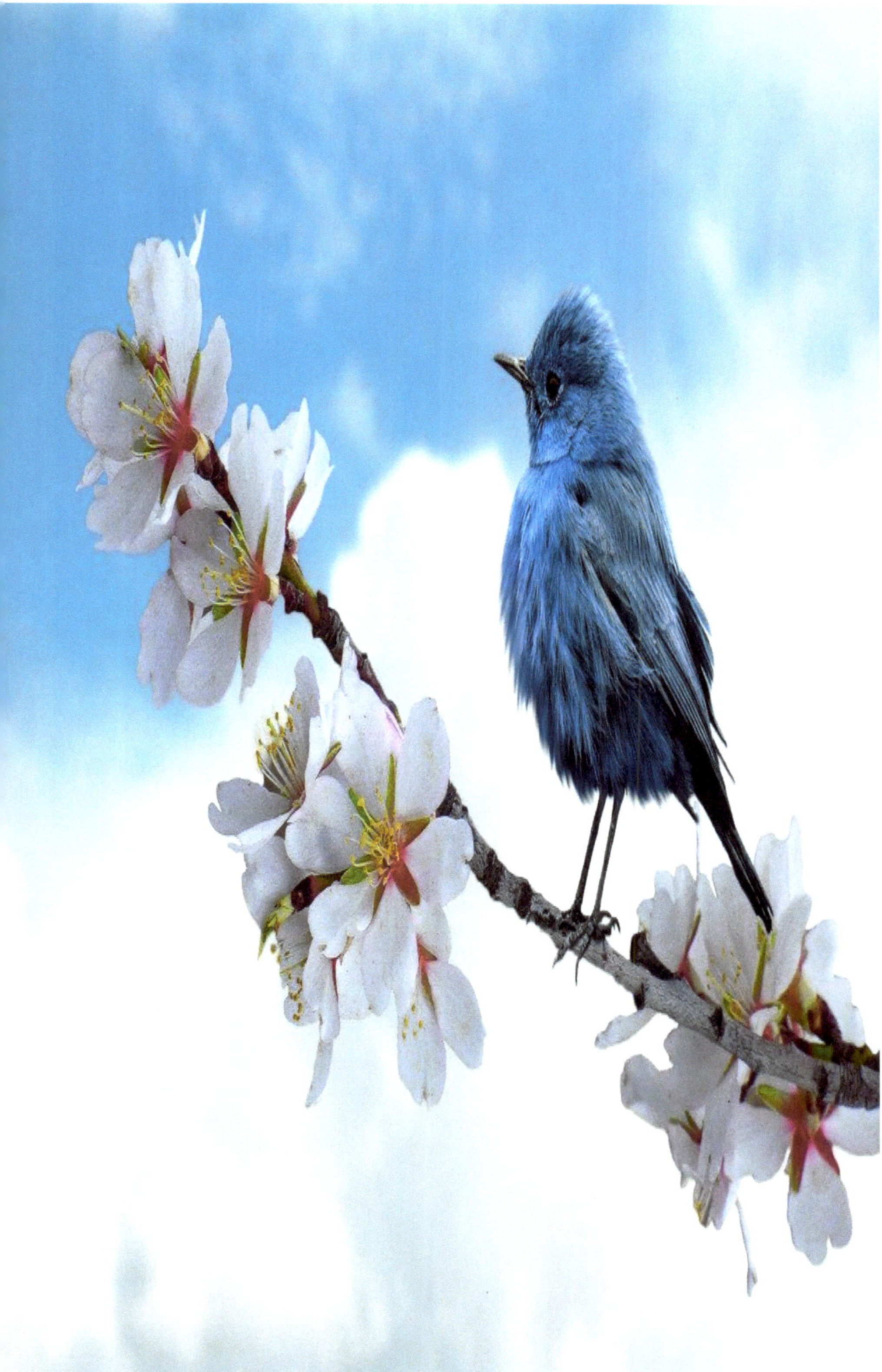

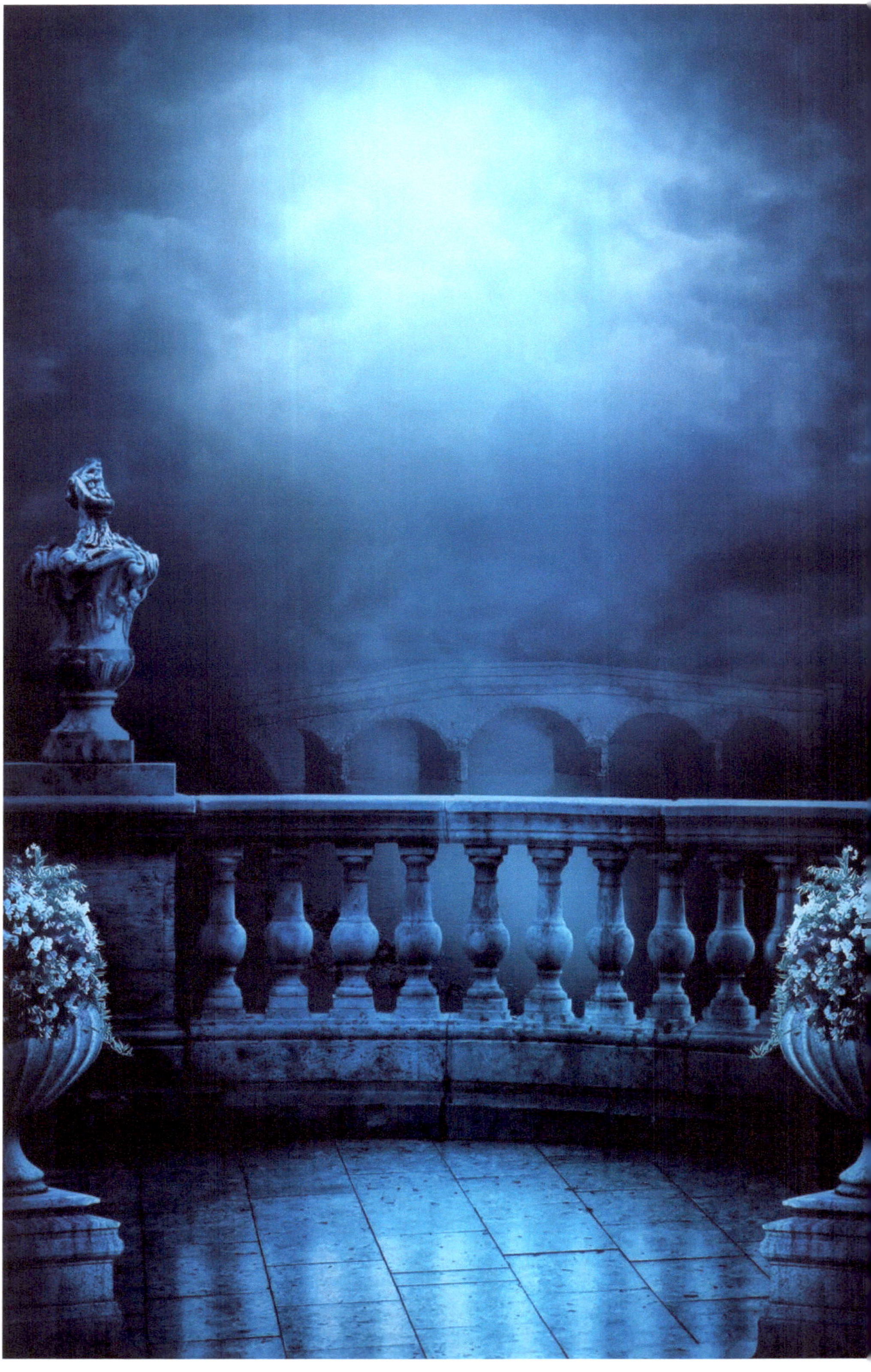

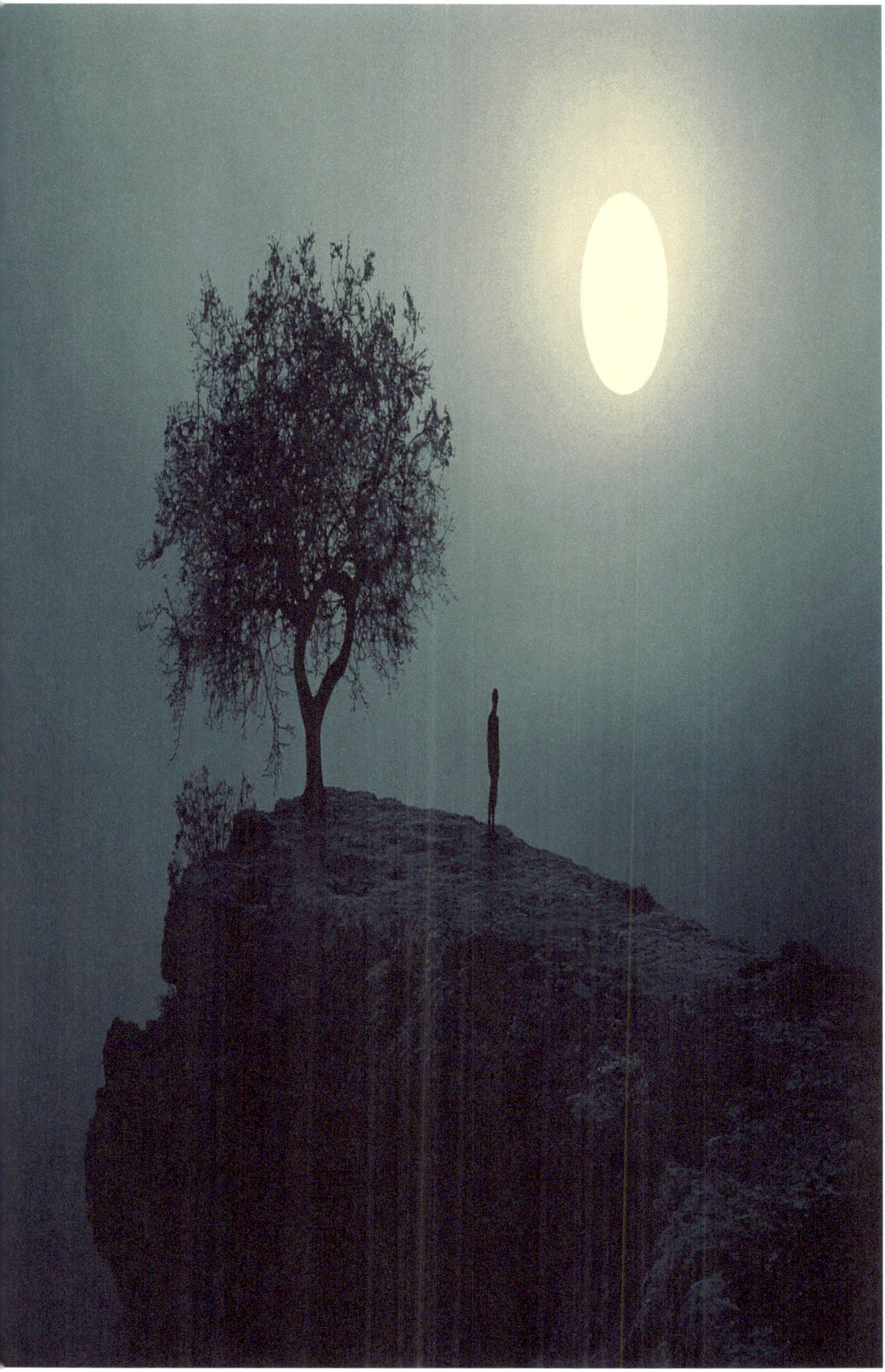

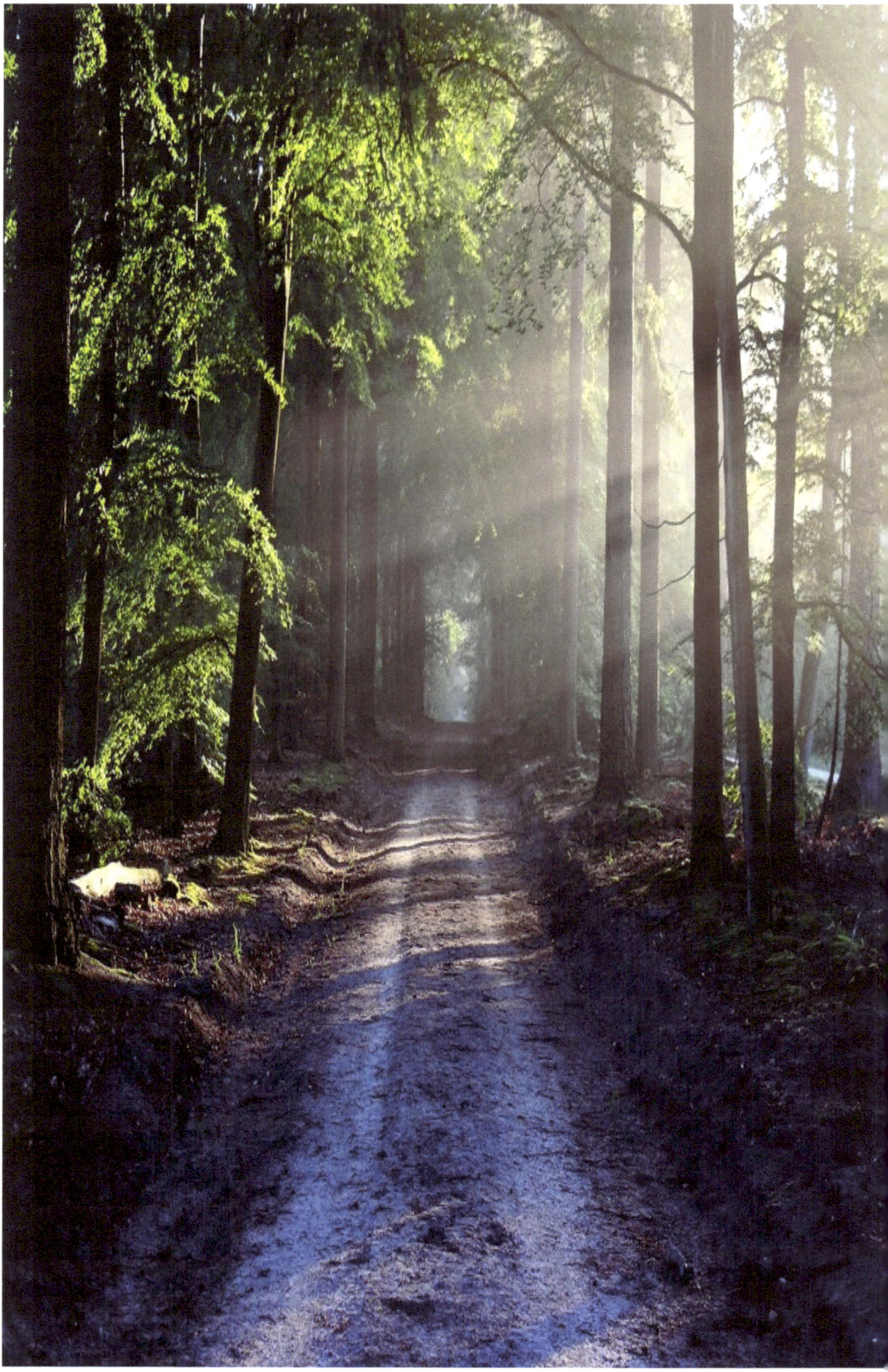

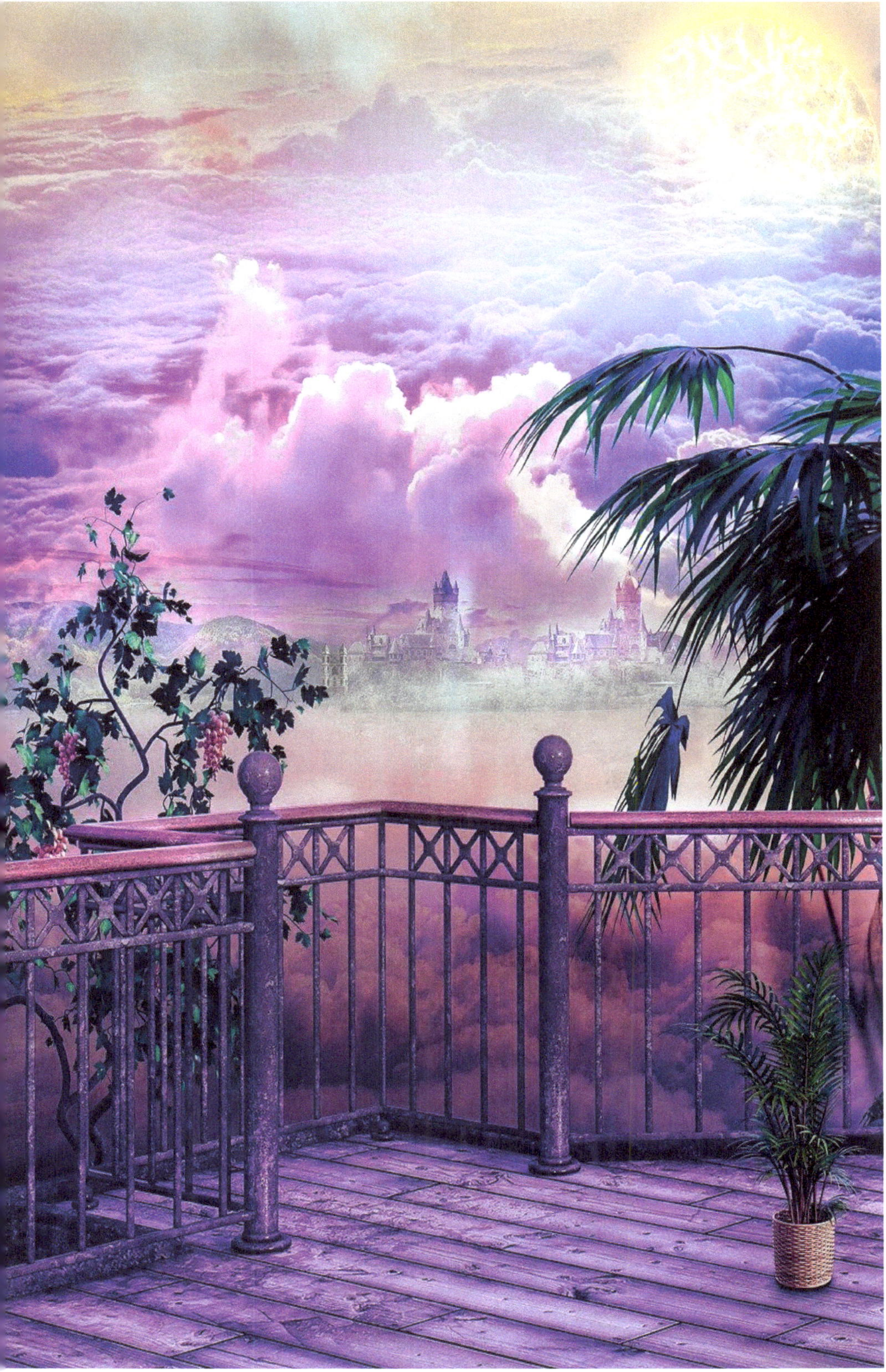

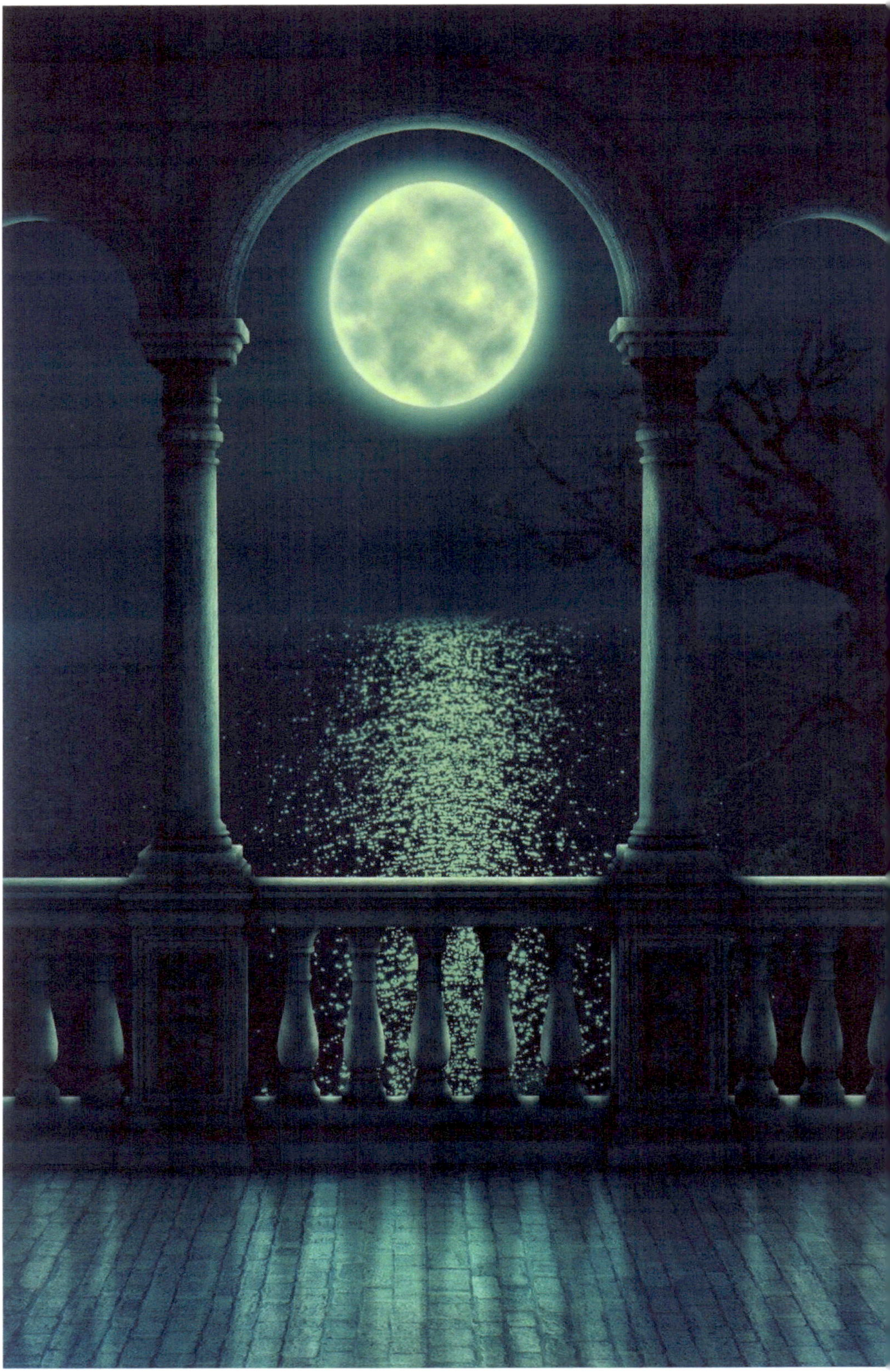

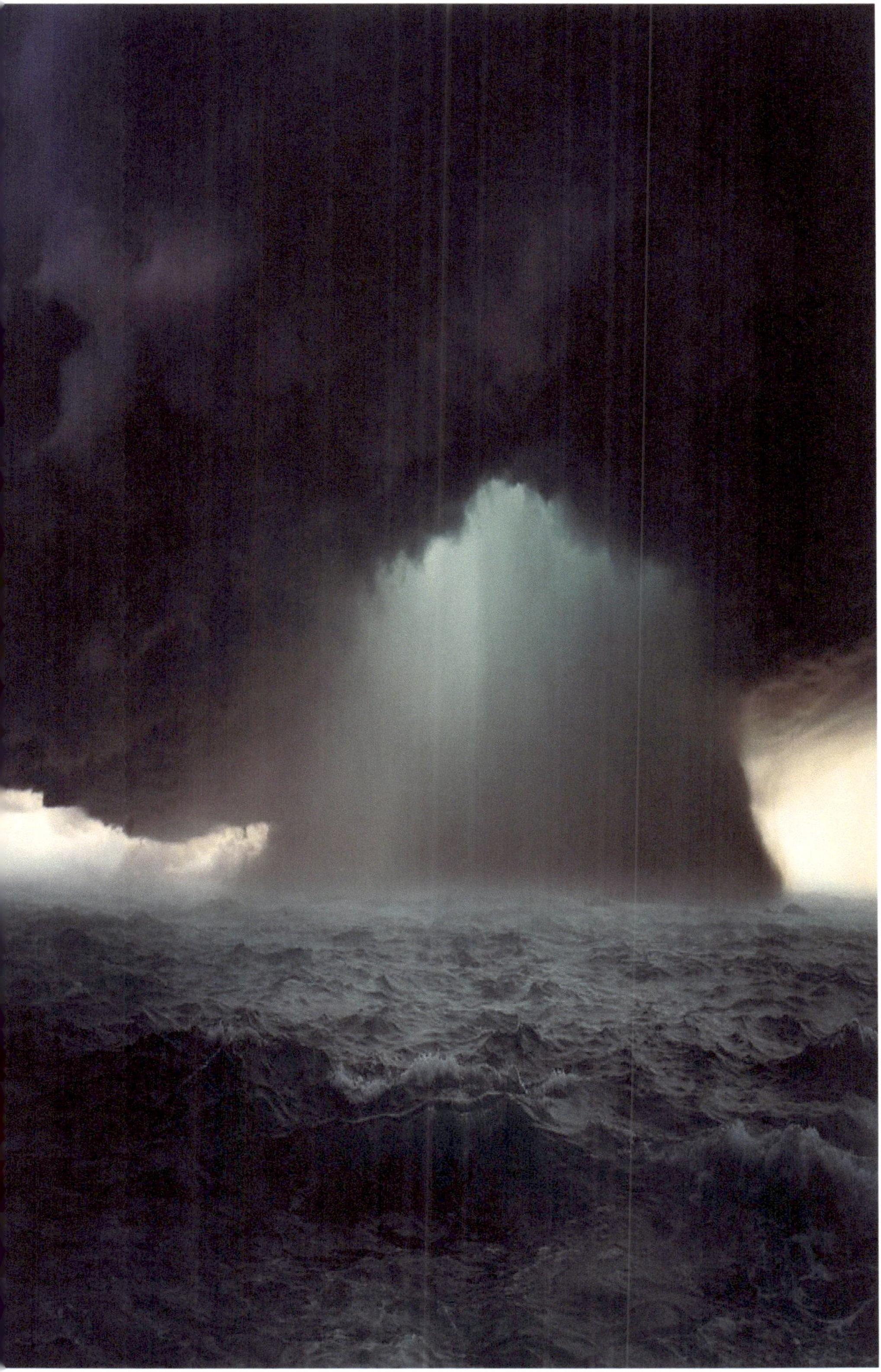

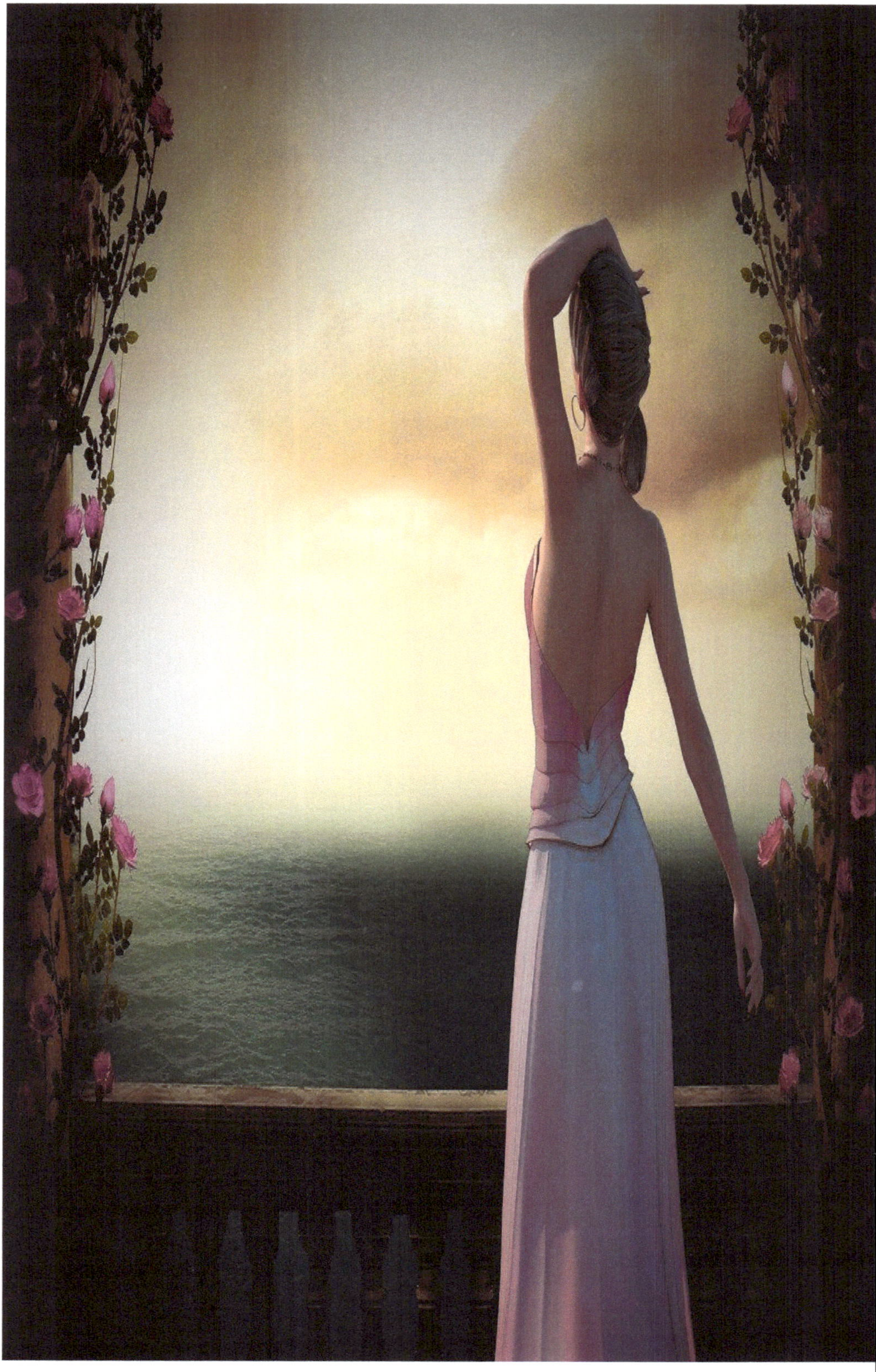

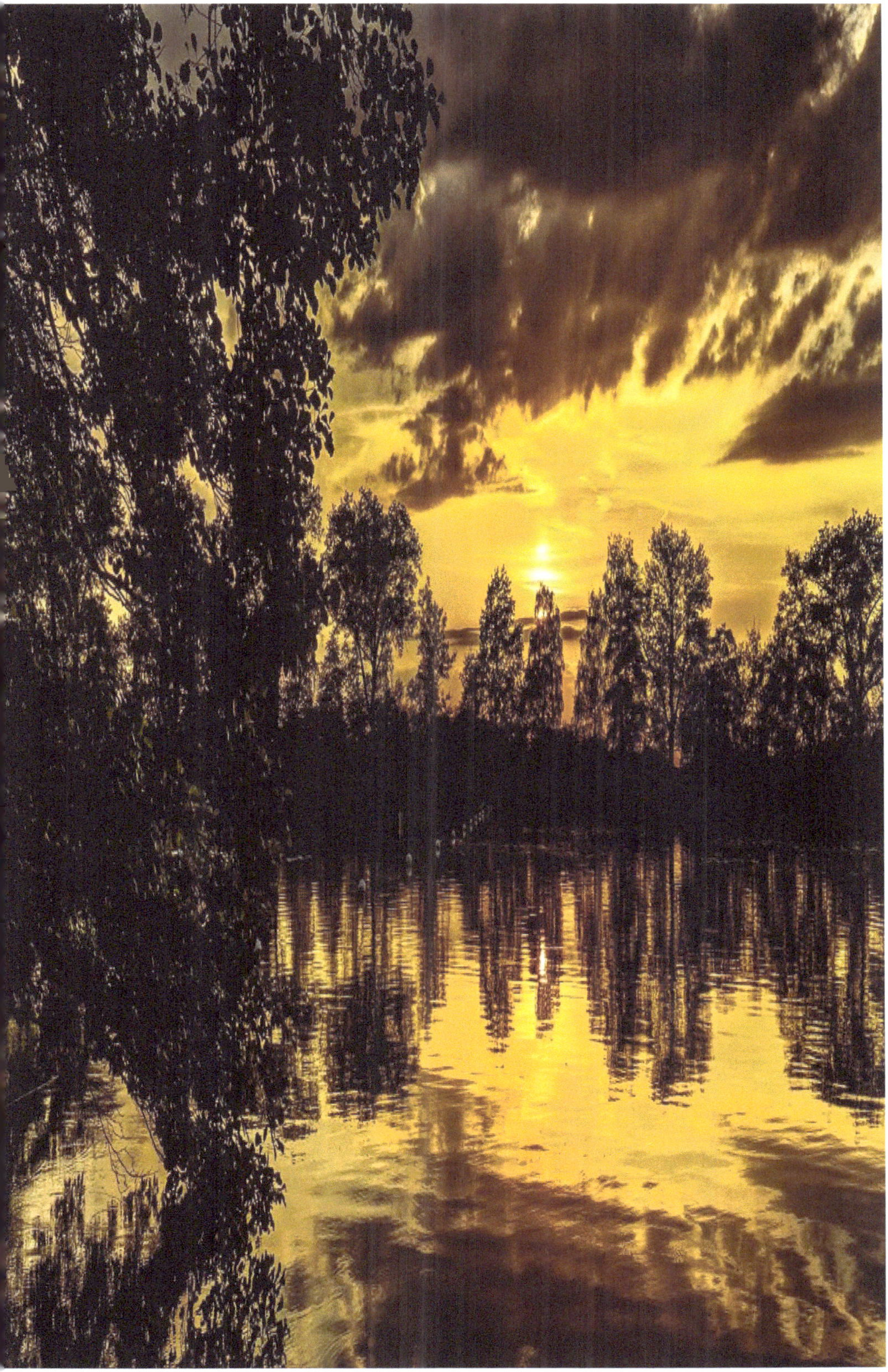

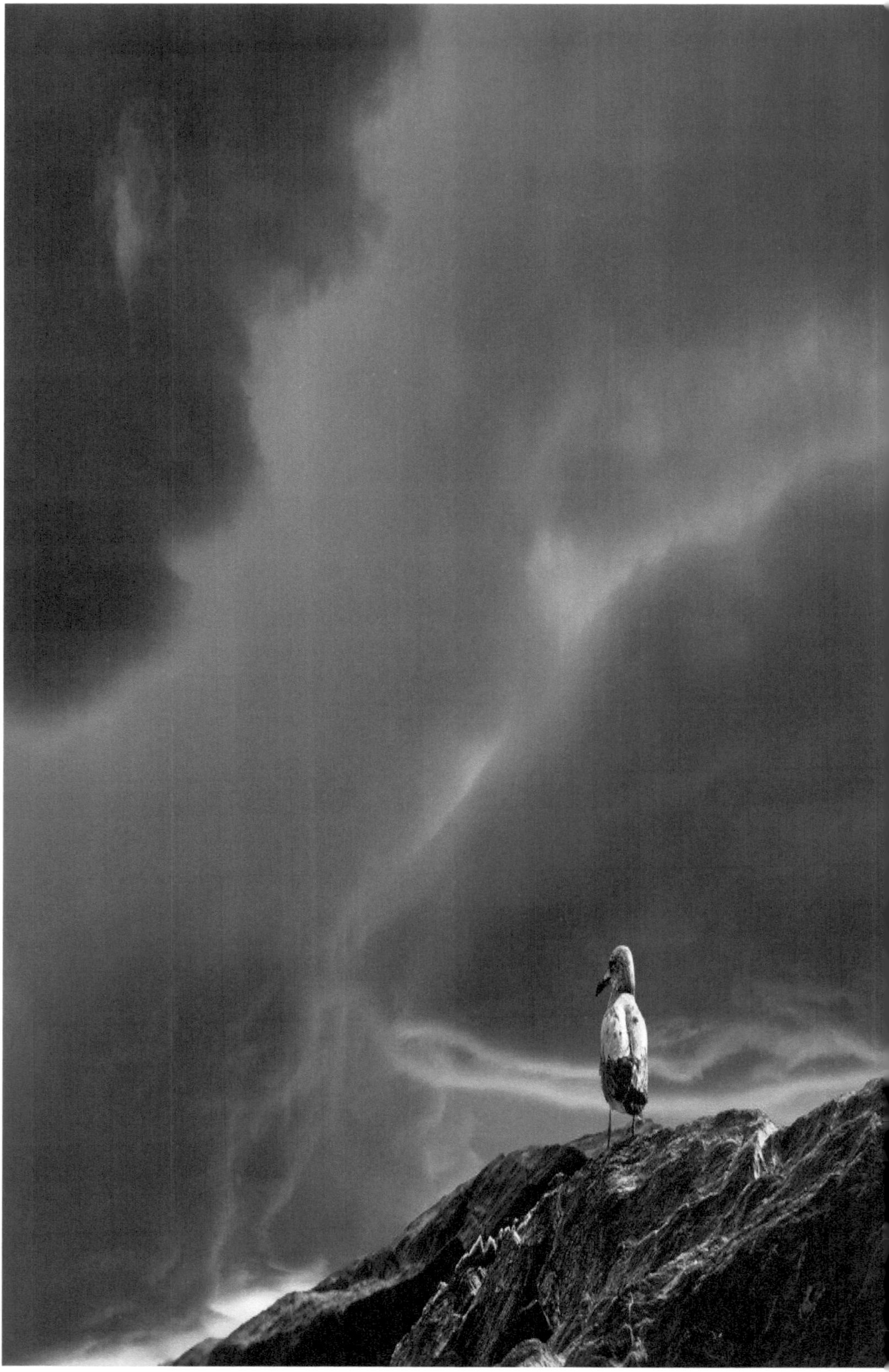

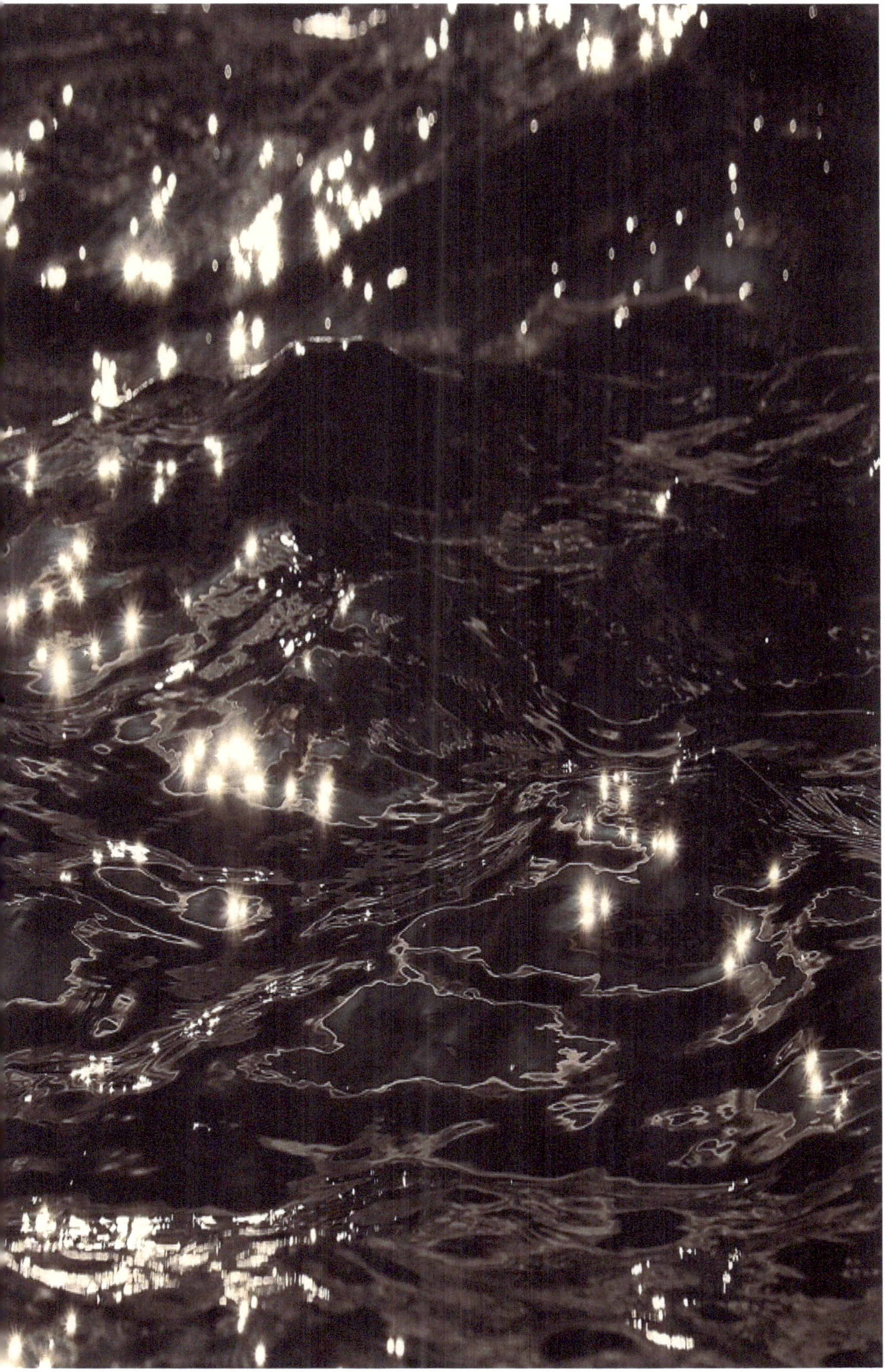

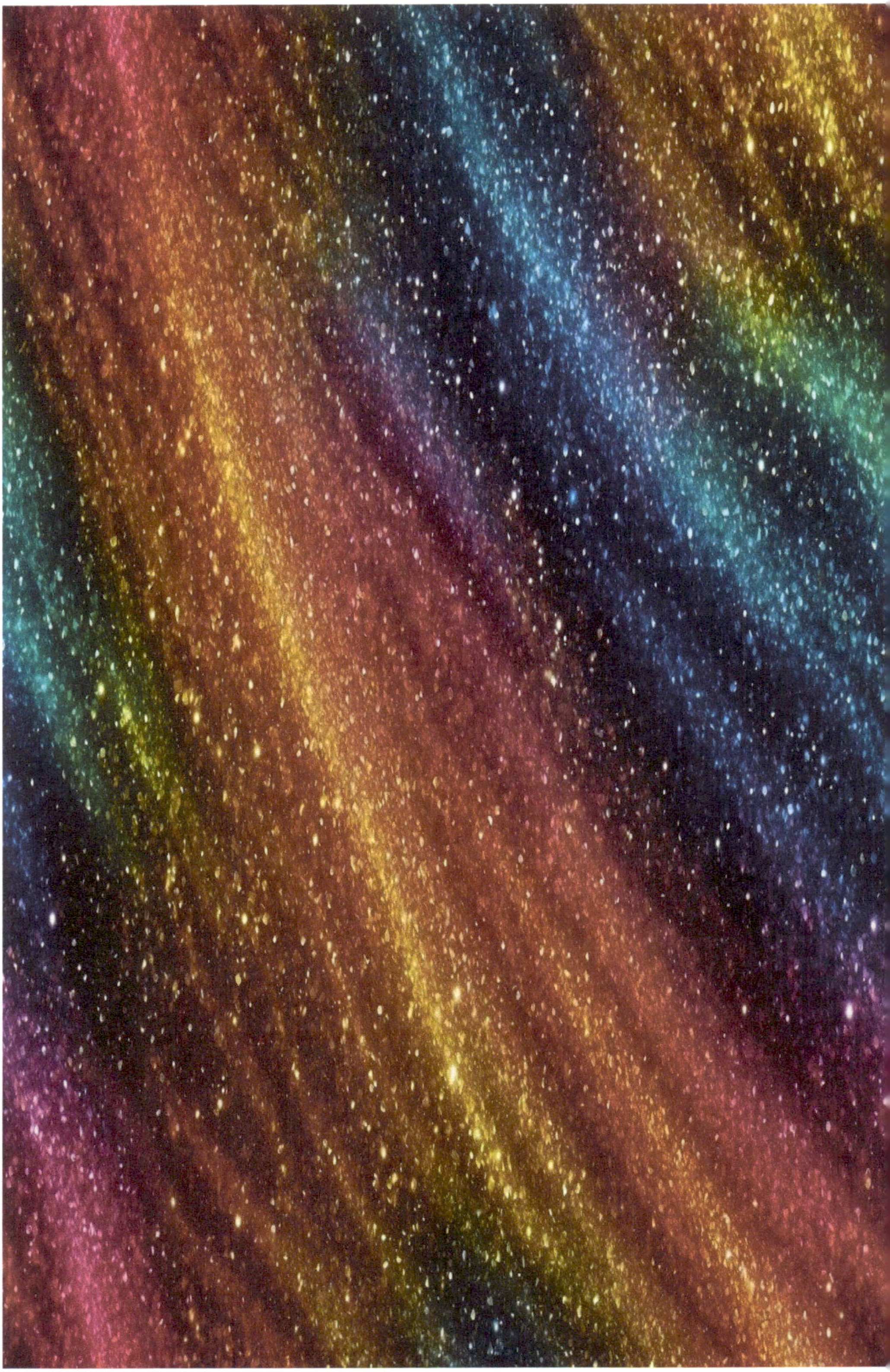

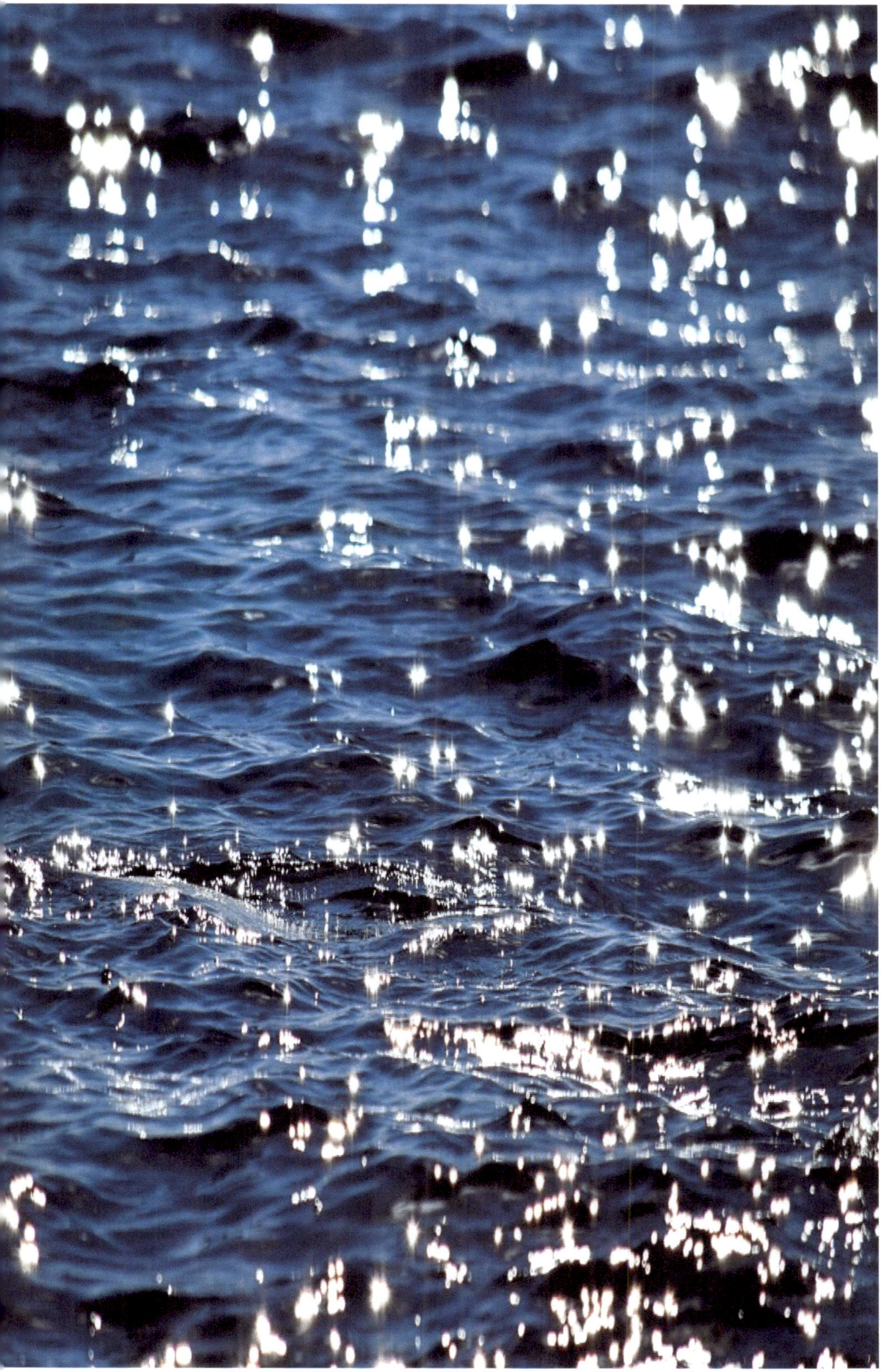

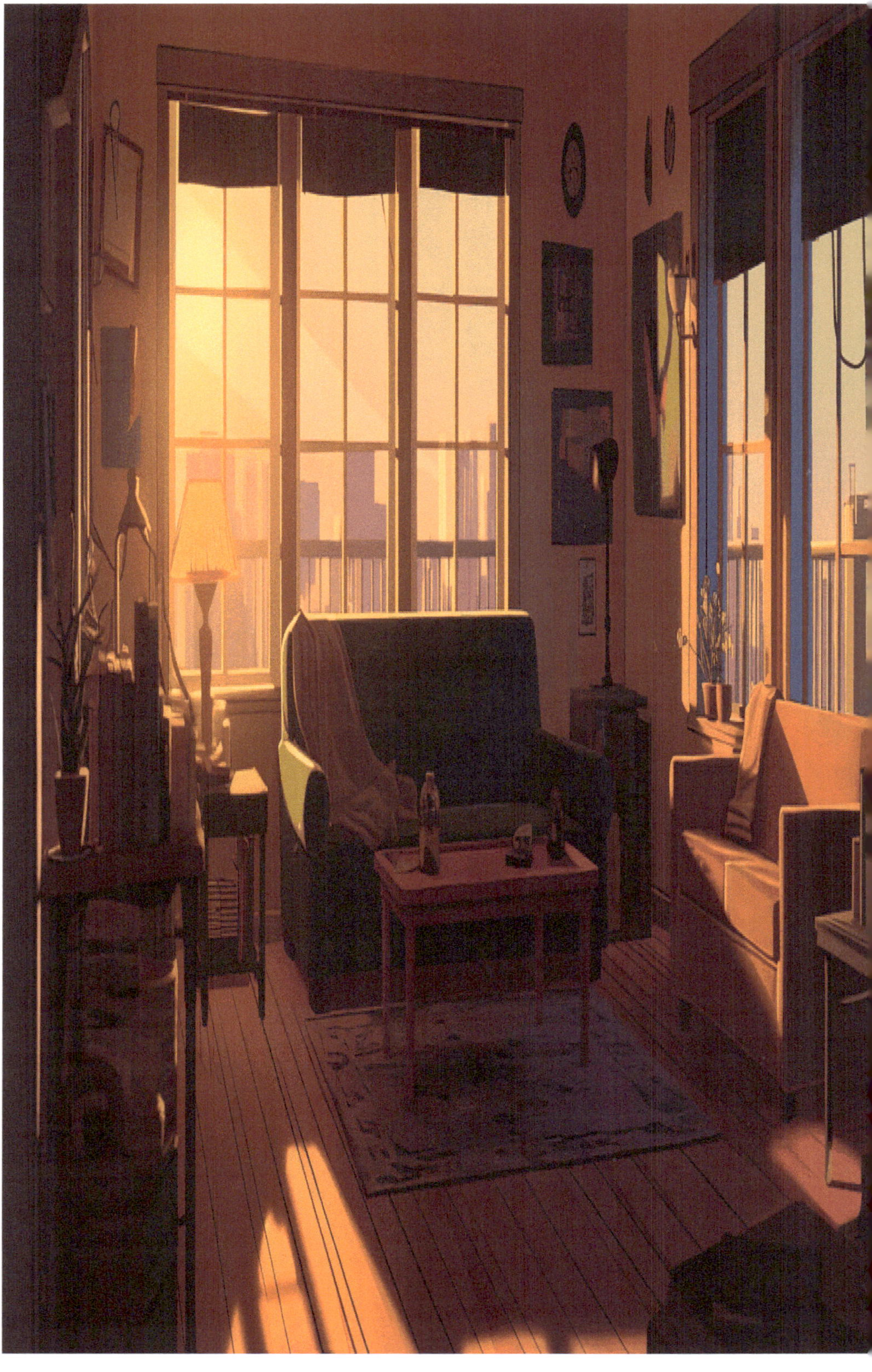

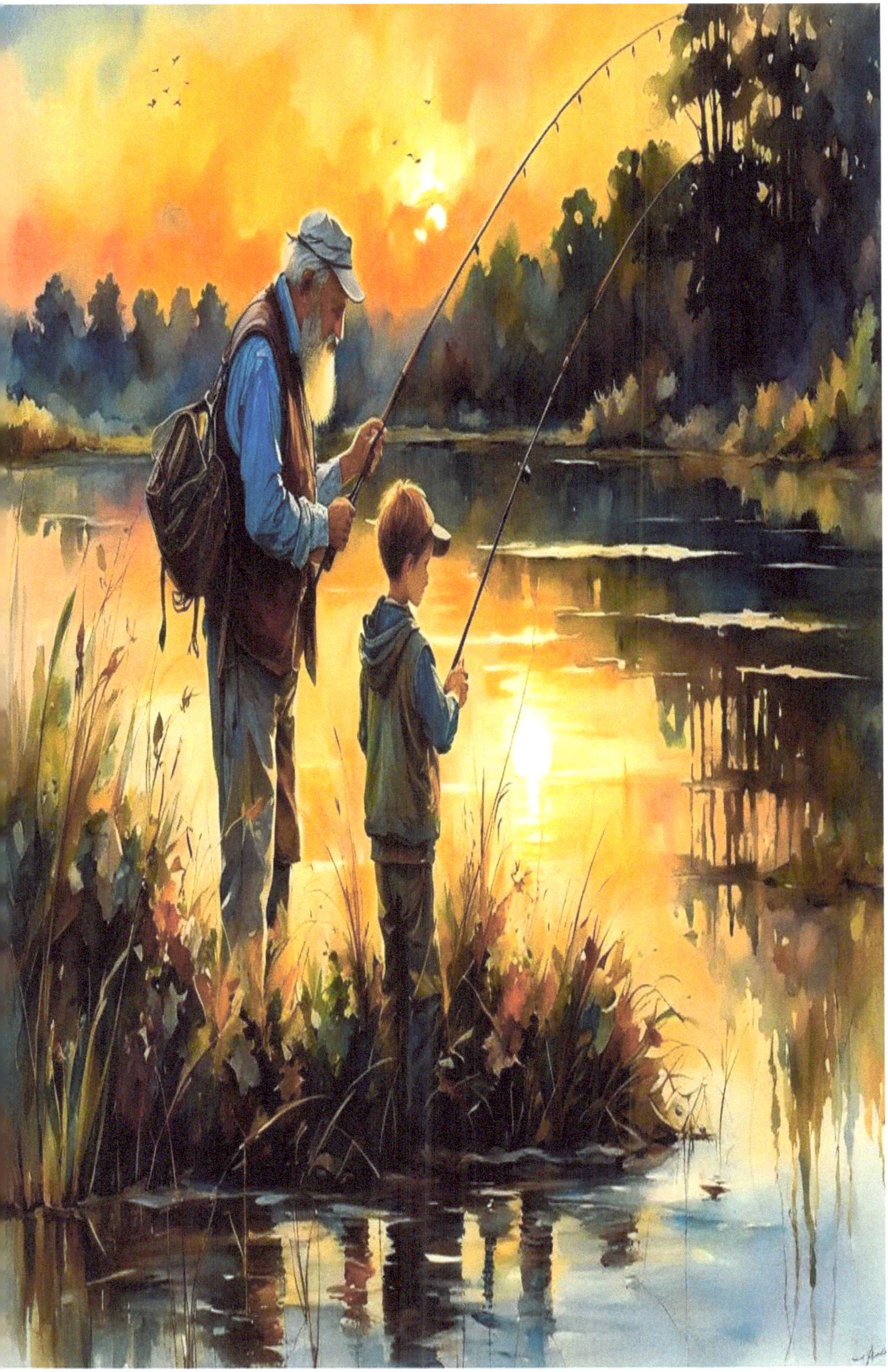

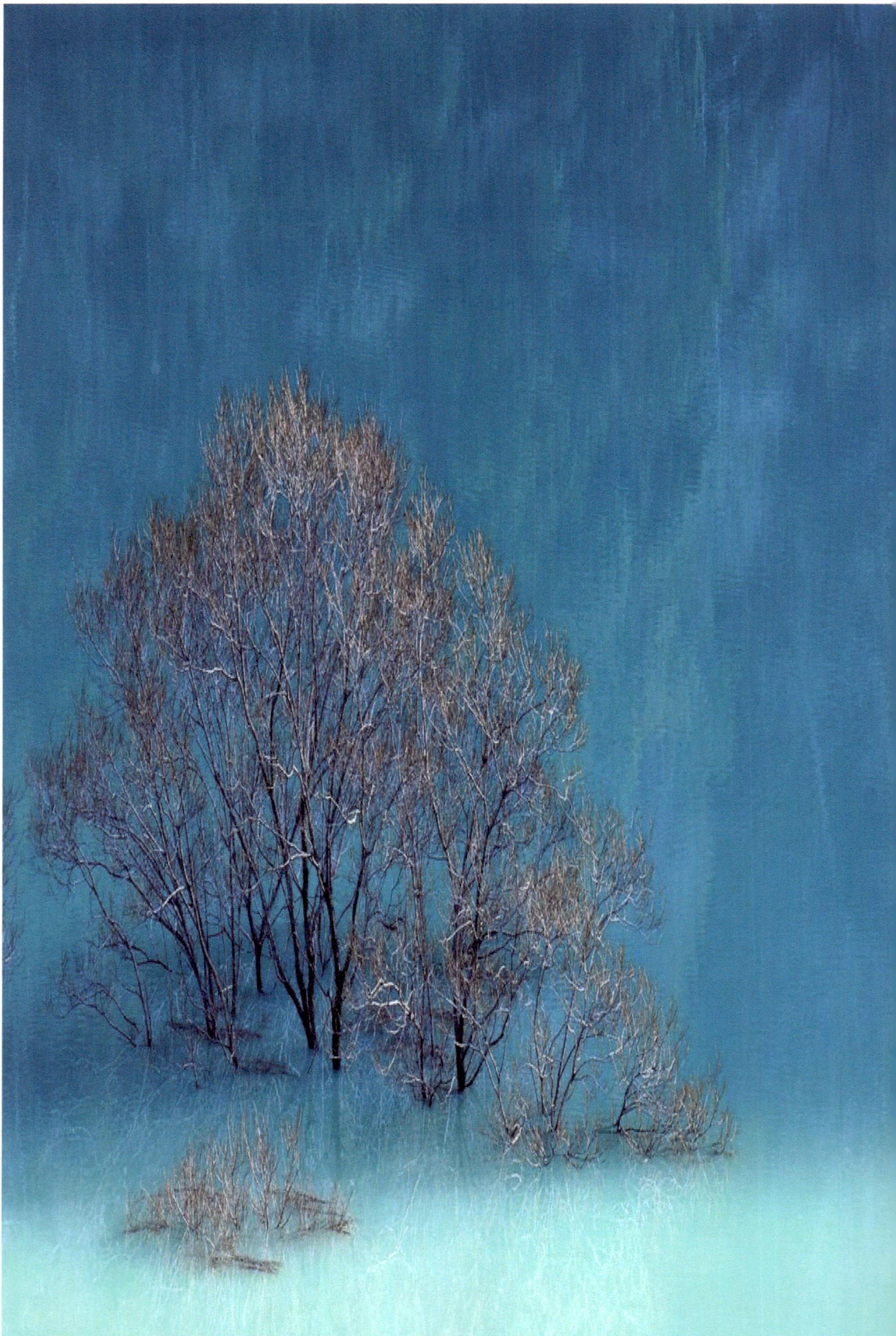

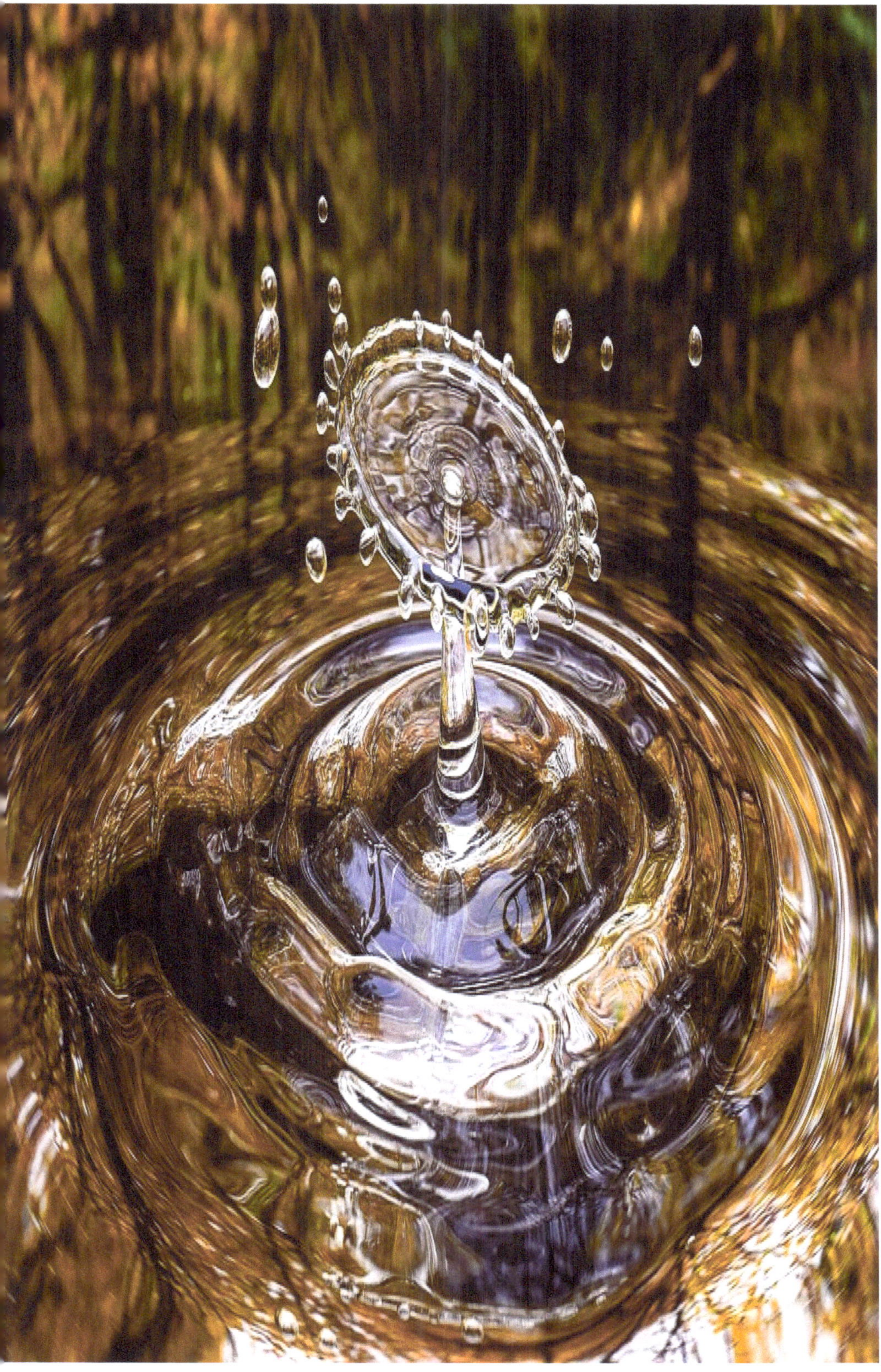

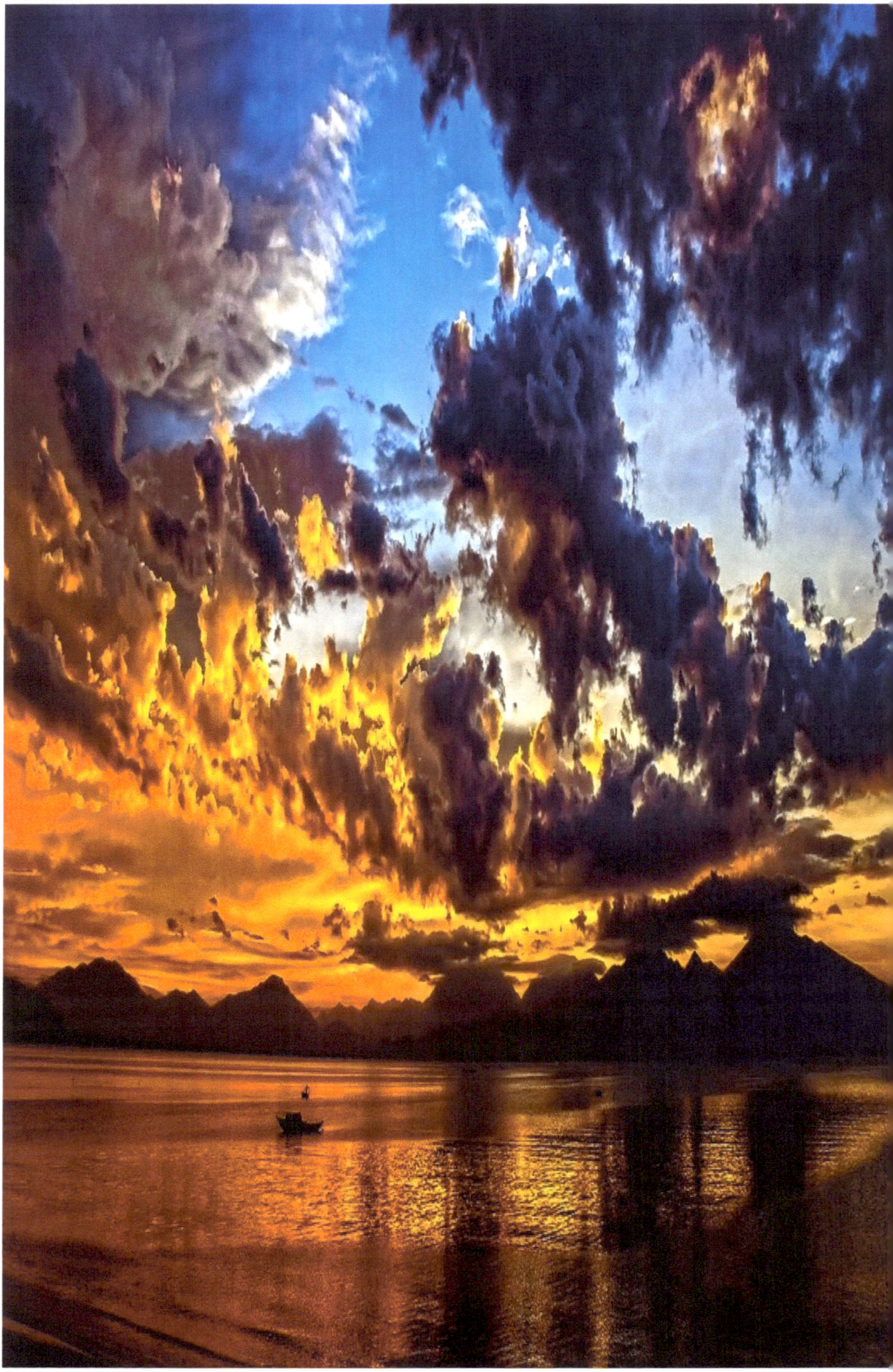

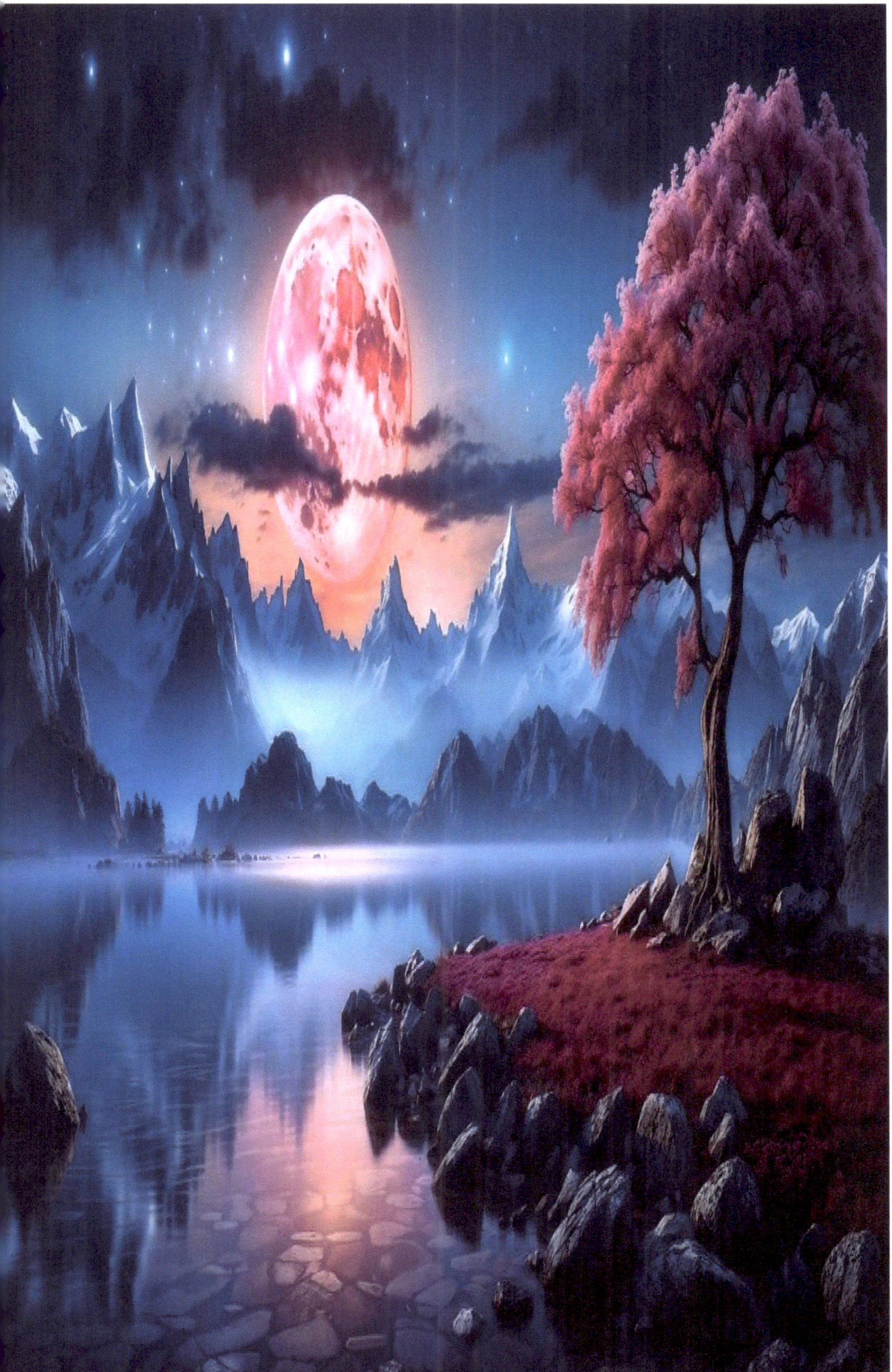

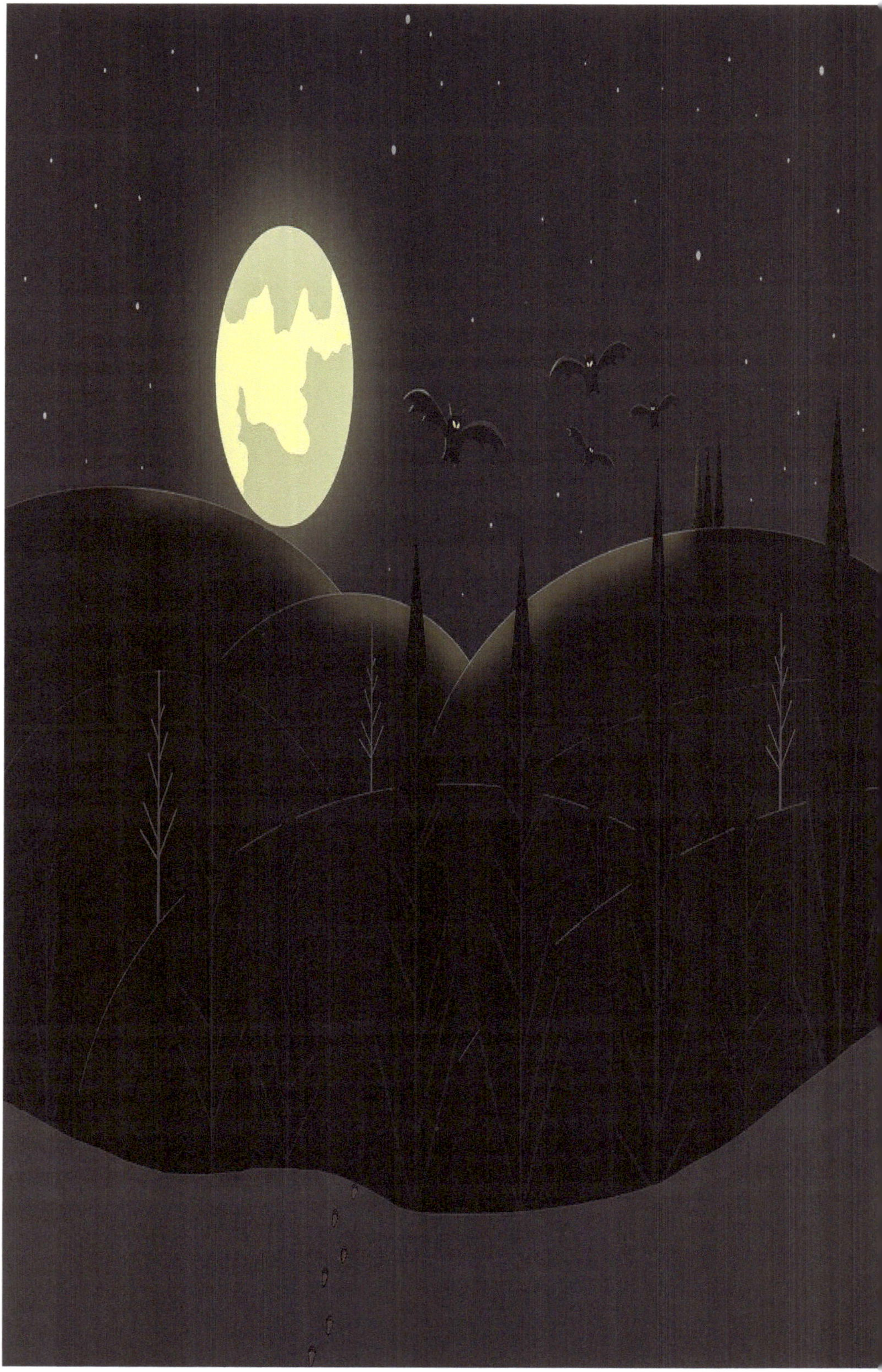

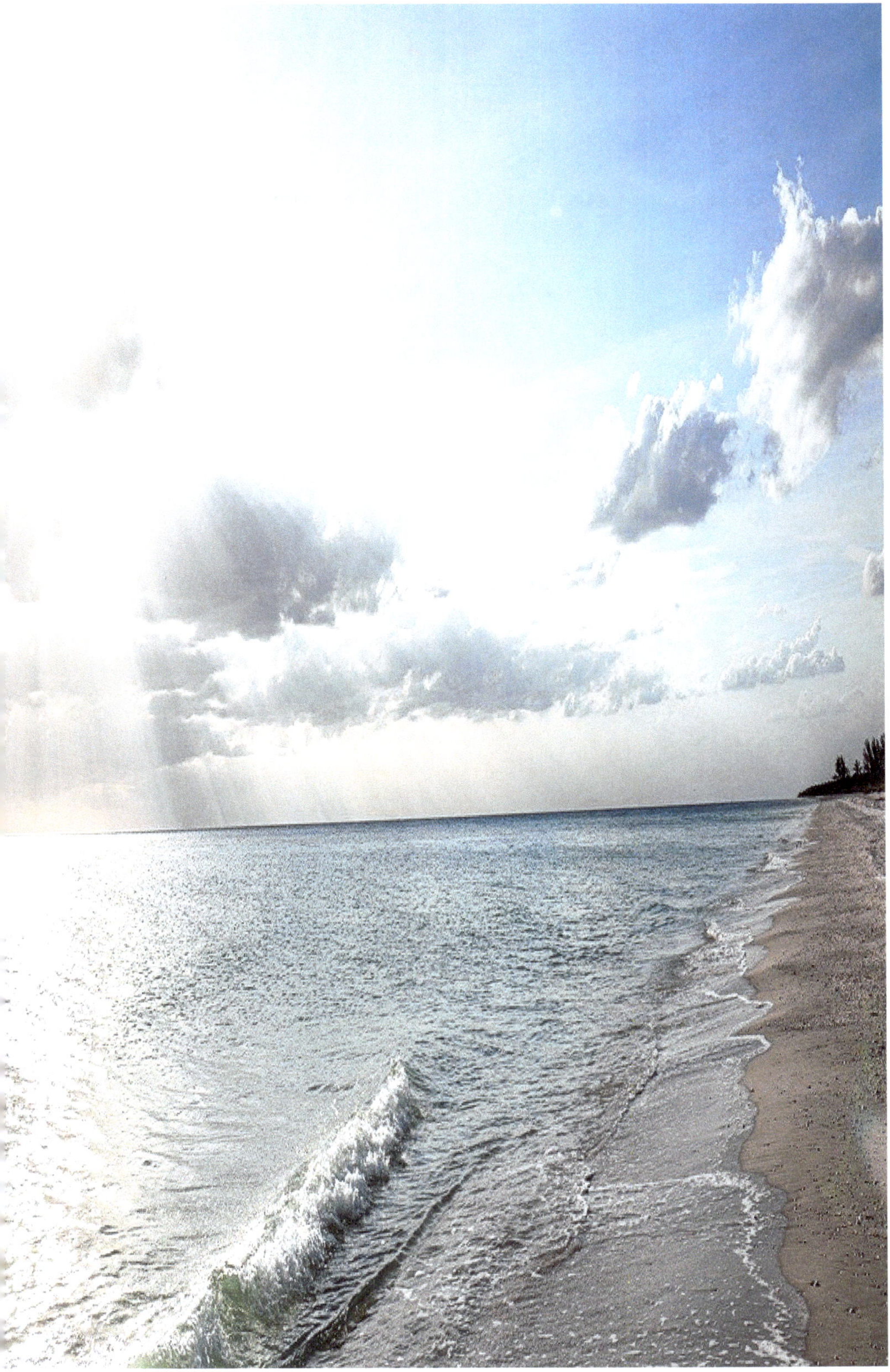

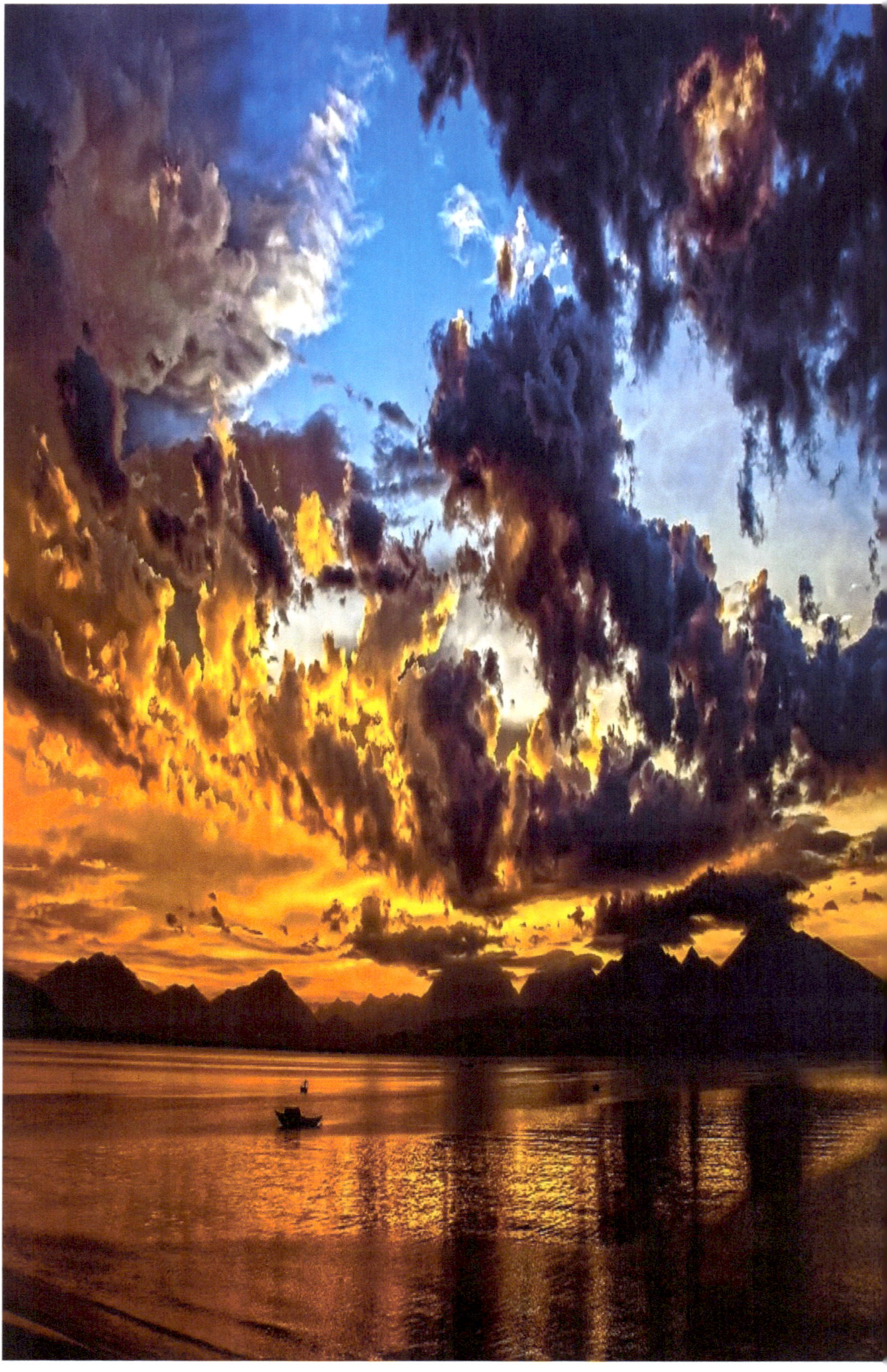

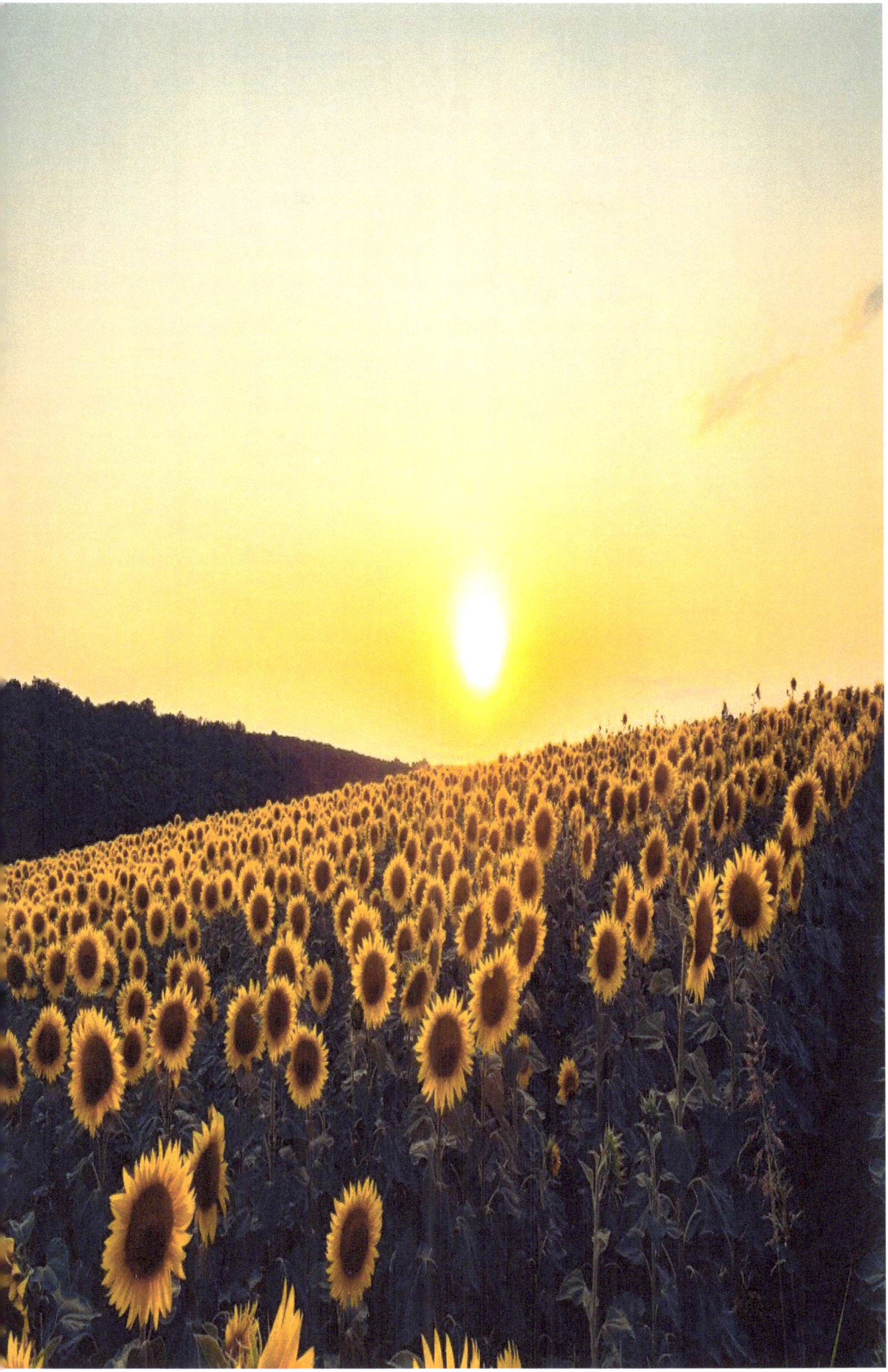

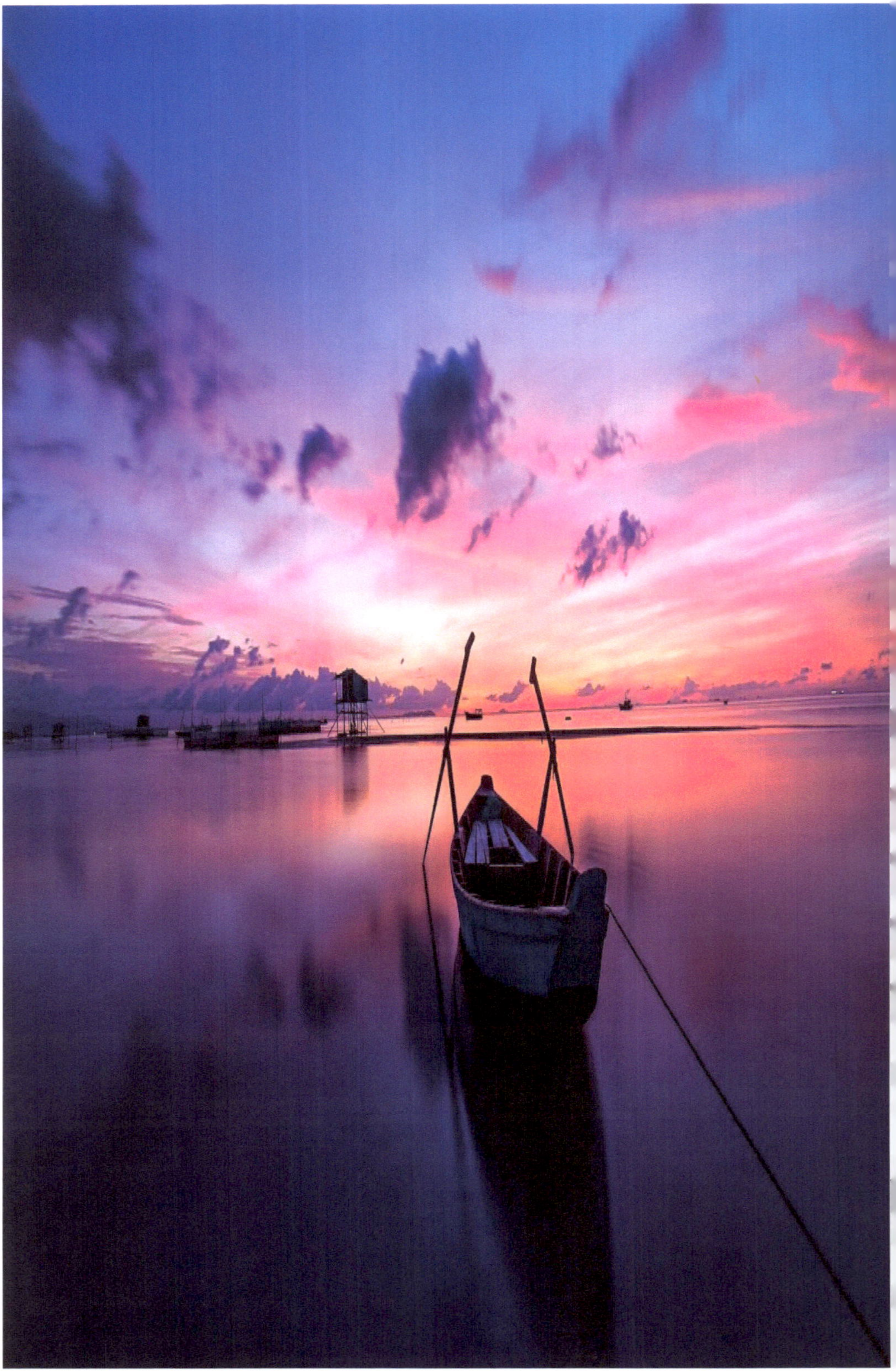

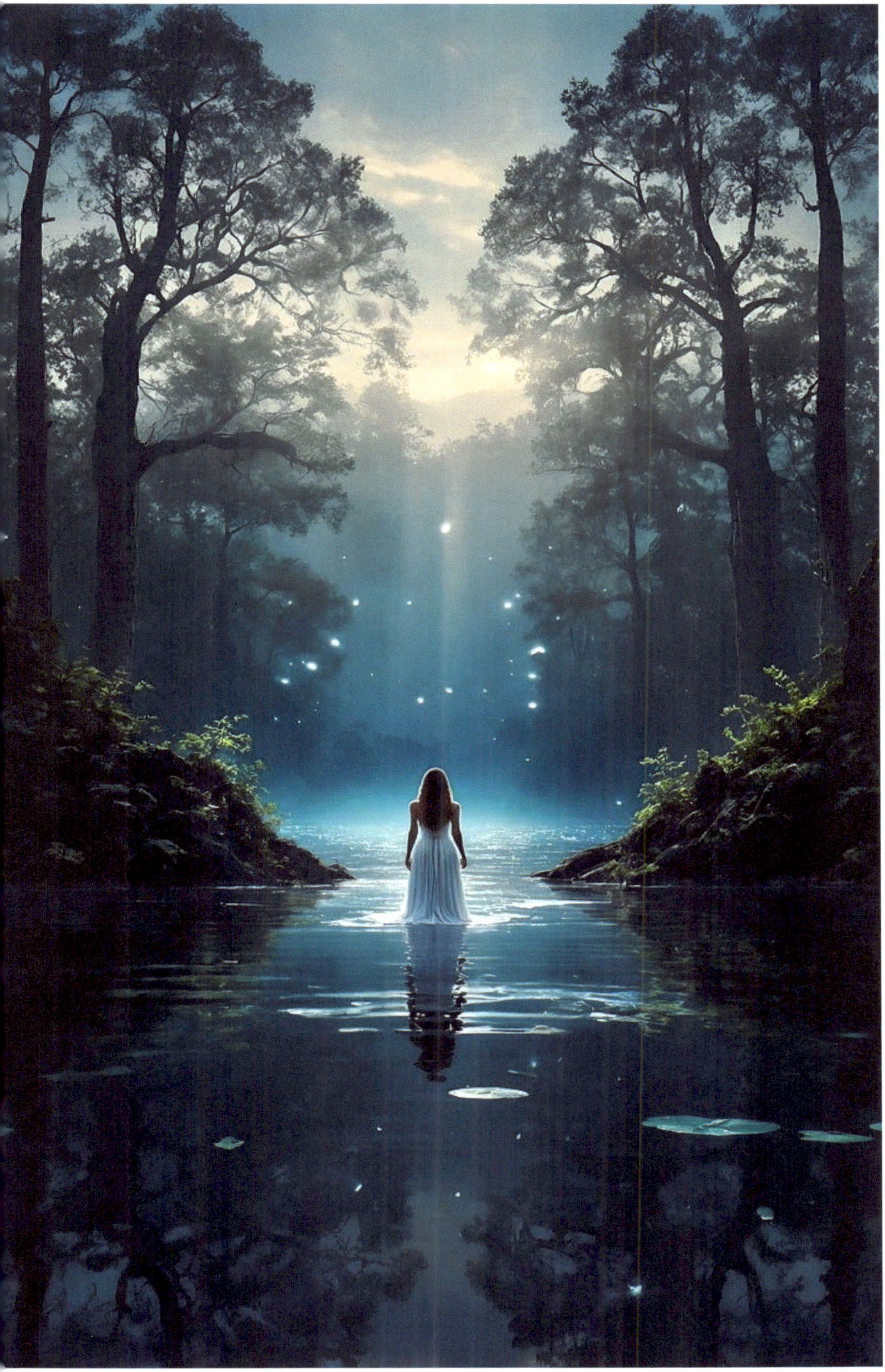

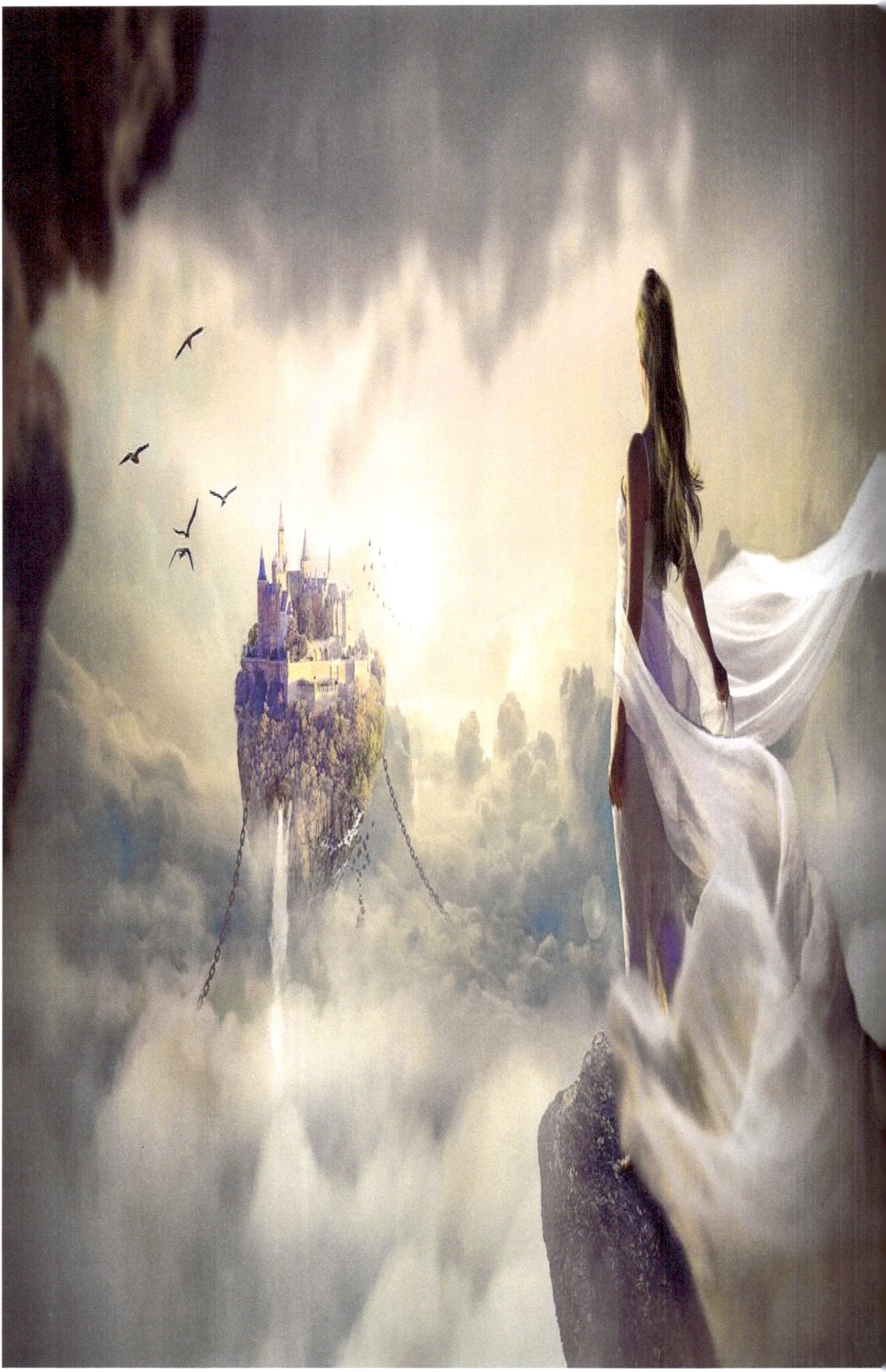

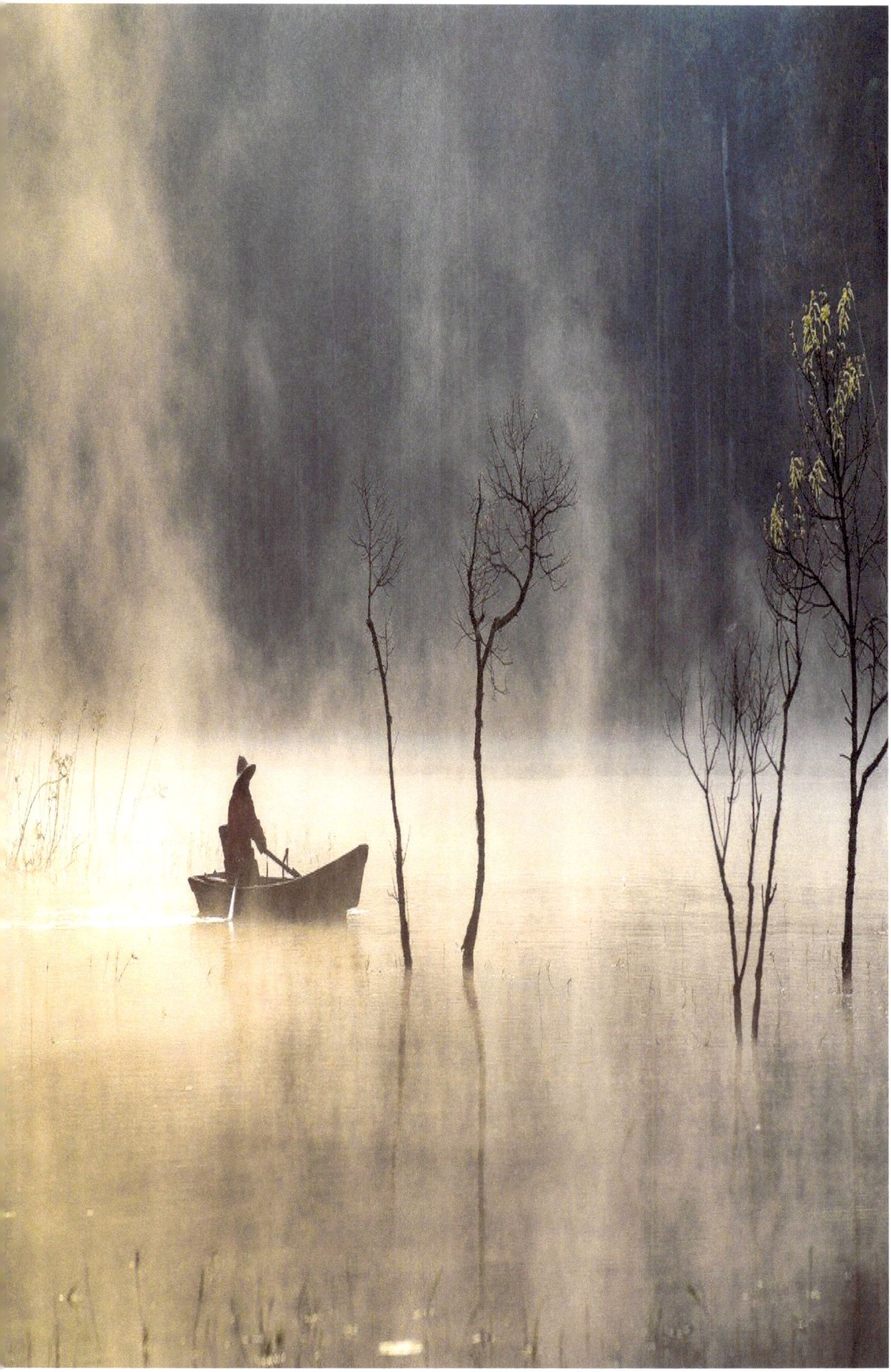

www.ingramcontent.com/pod-product-compliance
Lightning Source LLC
Chambersburg PA
CBHW040248220526
45473CB00001B/416
9798341437760